# The STALIN File

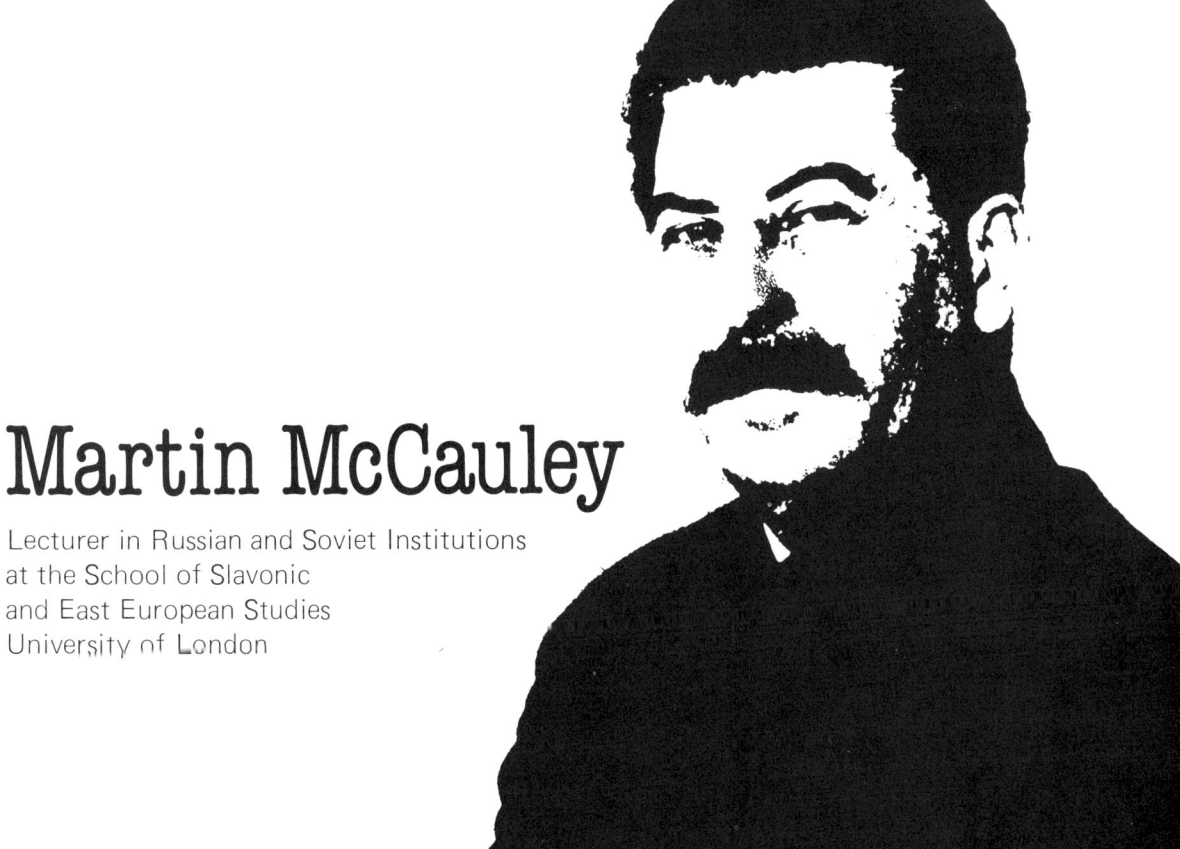

## Martin McCauley

Lecturer in Russian and Soviet Institutions
at the School of Slavonic
and East European Studies
University of London

B T Batsford Ltd  London

# File notes on Joseph Stalin

| 1 FAMILY NAME | GIVEN NAME | MIDDLE NAME(S) |
|---|---|---|
| Djugashvili | Joseph | Vissarionovich |

**2 ALIASES AND PSEUDONYMS**

J Besoshvili/Chizhikov/David/Ivanov/Ivanovich/K Kato/Ko./Koba/K St./Gaioz Nizharadze/Ryaboi/Soselo/Soso/ *STALIN*/Zakhar Gregorian Melikyants/Vasily/Vasilyev

**3 NATIONALITY**

Georgian. Citizen of the Union of Soviet Socialist Republics (USSR)

| 4 PLACE OF BIRTH | 5 DATE OF BIRTH |
|---|---|
| Gori, Georgia, the Caucasus | 21 December 1879 |

| 6 PLACE OF DEATH | 7 DATE OF DEATH |
|---|---|
| Moscow, USSR | 5 March 1953 |

| 8 FATHER | 9 MOTHER |
|---|---|
| Vissarion Ivanovich Djugashvili, shoemaker, born 18?  died 1890 | Ekaterina Georgievna Djugashvili (née Geladze), born 1855 died 1936 |

**10 BROTHERS AND SISTERS**

Three born before Stalin, all died shortly after birth

**11 MARITAL DETAILS**

Married Ekaterina Svanidze in February 1904, died in 1909, of pneumonia
Married Nadezhda Alliluyeva in 1918, committed suicide, 8 November 1932

**12 CHILDREN**

Yakov, born 16 March 1908, died in Sachsenhausen concentration camp, Germany, 1943
Vasily, born 1920, died 1962
Svetlana, born 1926

**13 DESCRIPTION (AT 60 YEARS)**

| HEIGHT | BUILD | HAIR | FACE | COMPLEXION | EYES |
|---|---|---|---|---|---|
| 2 arshins, 4½ vershki (5 ft 4 ins; 1.63 metres) | Average Strongly and squarely built | Straight Dark brown (greying) Moustache and beard reddish-brown (greying) | Flat forehead, not high Long, straight nose Sharp chin | Sallow Covered with smallpox marks | Dark brown |

**14 PECULIARITIES**

Front molar missing in the right lower jaw
Birthmark on left ear
Second and third toes of left foot joined together

**15 MAJOR POLITICAL/MILITARY POSTS HELD**

Commissar for Nationalities in Lenin's government, Nov 1917-July 1923
Secretary General of the Communist Party, April 1922-March 1953
Chairman of the Council of People's Commissars, May 1941-March 1953
Chairman of the State Committee of Defence, June 1941-1945
People's Commissar for War, July 1941-February 1946
Commander-in-Chief of Soviet Armed Forces, July 1941-1945
Marshal of the Armed Forces of the USSR, March 1943-1953

For Elizabeth, Timothy and Richard Moss

First published 1979
© text Martin McCauley 1979
Typeset by Tek-Art Ltd S.E.20
Printed by The Anchor Press Ltd, Tiptree, Essex
for the Publishers, B.T. Batsford Ltd,
4 Fitzhardinge Street, London W1H 0AH

ISBN 0 7134 1918 0

## Acknowledgment

The Author and Publishers thank the following for permission to use the pictures in this book: *Daily Mail*, fig. 38; the Imperial War Museum, for fig. 33; the Mansell Collection, for the frontispiece and figs. 1, 3, 8, 15, 16, 37; Novosti Press Agency, for figs. 4, 7, 9, 12, 13, 14, 17, 18, 27, 30, 36, 42, 43; Radio Times Hulton Picture Library, for figs. 5, 6, 19, 28, 31, 50, 51, 52; Rex Features Ltd, for figs. 34, 40, 45; United Press International Ltd, for figs. 20, 44.

Frontispiece: Painting by Irakly Toidze: Stalin as Military Leader, standing in the Kremlin.

# Contents

# Note on Old Style and New Style Dates

Until February 1918 the Russians used a different system of dating from other Europeans. The Russians used the Julian Calendar (named after Julius Caesar), which had been adopted by most West European countries in the 6th century. However, an error had been discovered in it, and in 1582 Pope Gregory XIII introduced a new calendar (known ever since as the Gregorian Calendar) which was gradually adopted by the countries of Europe. Russia did not adopt the Gregorian Calendar because the Russian Orthodox Church, the official state church, did not accept the Roman Catholic Pope's authority to decide dates.

The error in the Julian Calendar grew larger each century. In the nineteenth century (1800-1899) the difference between a Julian Calendar (Old Style) date and a Gregorian Calendar (New Style) date was 12 days. In the twentieth century (from 1900 onwards) the difference between a Julian Calendar (Old Style) date and a Gregorian Calendar (New Style) date was 13 days.

Therefore, if you want to discover the New Style date for an Old Style date in the nineteenth century, you should add twelve days. For example, Alexander II was assassinated on 1 March 1881 (Old Style) — which means 13 (1 + 12) March 1881 (New Style). If you want to discover the New Style date for an Old Style one in the twentieth century, then you should add 13 days. For example, the October Revolution broke out on 25 October 1917 (Old Style) — which means 7 November 1917 (New Style). This is why you will sometimes find the October Revolution referred to as the "November Revolution". In the same way, the February Revolution, which took place at the end of February 1917 (Old Style), and therefore in March 1917 (New Style), is sometimes referred to as the "March Revolution".

*In this book all dates are New Style.* Therefore you do not need to add any days to discover what the date in our country was at the same time. There are two exceptions to this: the February and the October Revolutions of 1917. To describe these Revolutions, the Old Style months have been used because in the Soviet Union today this is the usual way of describing the two revolutions. Because to describe the Revolutions in this way does not match the use of the New Style system of dating everywhere else in the book, the "February Revolution" and the "October Revolution" are put in inverted commas.

The Russians adopted the Gregorian Calendar on 1 February 1918, which therefore became 14 February. From then on Russian dates were the same as European ones.

# Chapter One  1879-1924

# Stalin's Early Political Activities, Through the 1917 Revolutions, and up to the Death of Lenin

## Stalin's Early Political Activities

On page 70 there is a List of Dates of Stalin's Activities. If you look at the section headed "Early Political Activities" one thing will certainly strike you: Stalin spent much of his youth in prison or in exile for *illegal political activities*.* In 1908 Stalin was imprisoned in Baku. A fellow prisoner there, called Semya Vereshchak, described Stalin's arrival in Baku in an *émigré* journal years later. Stalin joined the group of prisoners who were *Bolsheviks:*

> One day a new face appeared in the Bolshevik camp. I enquired who the comrade was, and in great secrecy was told: "It is Koba [Stalin] .... Koba stood out among the various circles as a *Marxist* student. He wore a blue satin smock with a wide open collar and no belt. His head was bare. A bashlik — a sort of detached hood with two tapering scarves — was thrown across his shoulders. He always carried a book. Of more than medium height, he walked with a slow, cat-like tread. He was slender, with a pointed face, pock-marked skin, sharp nose, small eyes peering out from a narrow forehead, slightly indented. He spoke little and sought no company.

*For more details about *illegal political activities* turn to the Glossary, page 88. All words which are covered in the Glossary are printed in italics when they are first mentioned in the book.

Koba was one of the many names by which Stalin (as we now refer to him) was known during his life. There is a list of all his pseudonyms and aliases on page 76.

## The 1917 Revolutions
## The "February Revolution"

Stalin was still in exile in Siberia when the "February Revolution" took place. The Revolution proved victorious: Tsar Nicholas II abdicated and his brother Mikhail refused to succeed him as Tsar. The government was officially taken over by the so-called *Provisional Government*, although the influence of the unofficial government, the *Petrograd Soviet of Workers' and Soldiers' Deputies* was just as great. Once the Revolution had proved victorious, Stalin and other revolutionaries made haste for Petrograd. Stalin had been co-opted as a member of the Central Committee (*CC*) of the Russian Social Democratic Labour Party (*RSDLP*) by Lenin in 1912, and this made him an important enough member of the party to take up a leading post on the party newspaper *Pravda*, when he arrived in Petrograd on 25 March 1917.

Stalin's power was relatively small at this time, even so. Stalin did not have as much influence as Lenin, the leader of the Bolsheviks. The Bolsheviks were not as big a number in the RSDLP in 1917 as their opponents, the *Mensheviks*. And the RSDLP (Bolsheviks and Mensheviks counted together) was not nearly as popular a party in Russia as the Socialist Revolutionary Party (*SRP*). The RSDLP based its strength on support from the industrial workers in Russia, while the SRP (whose policy was to transfer land held by landlords and the royal family to those who worked it with their own hands — in other words, to themselves) had the support of most agricultural workers and peasants. The population of Russia was about 160 million in 1917: 130 million were peasants; and only 4 million were industrial workers. If there had been a general election at this date, the RSDLP would have won very few seats in parliament.

However, by November 1917 the Bolsheviks had propelled themselves to power in Russia, and we shall see how Stalin also, from his humble beginnings, rose to a posi-tion of supreme power in the USSR.

## After the "February Revolution"

Everyone was excited by the Revolution and many believed that Russia was at last about to build a better tomorrow, a future of freedom from the rule of the Tsar and freedom from hunger and want. Stalin was not caught up in the fever of excitement. He kept calm and serious.

To begin with, Stalin and the Bolsheviks agreed with the Mensheviks that the working class was not capable of taking power immediately after the Revolution, and that an industrial country would have to be built up first. They therefore joined the Mensheviks in supporting the Provisional Government (the official government made up mainly of members of the *Duma* after it had been formally dissolved in February 1917)

rather than the Petrograd Soviet.

But when Lenin arrived in Petrograd from Switzerland in April 1917, he called for a change in Bolshevik policy. In his "April Theses" he said that it *was* possible for the working people and soldiers to seize power. His slogan was "All power to the *soviets*!" The Bolsheviks were shocked by this change in policy. Kamenev and Zinoviev openly expressed in the press their disagreement with Lenin's idea that the Bolsheviks should support the Petrograd Soviet and oppose the Provisional Government. Stalin, however, sided with Lenin, and was to do so on practically every issue until Lenin's death in 1924.

## The Provisional Government and the Petrograd Soviet

The Petrograd Soviet gained influence after March, while the Provisional Government's authority was heeded less and less. The Provisional Government was unsure of itself. It had not been elected, whereas the Petrograd Soviet had been elected by the workers and soldiers in Petrograd. The table here shows how the two governments differed slightly in their policies about the war and handing land over to the peasants.

## The Bolsheviks gain influence

The number of Bolsheviks in the Petrograd Soviet quickly rose. The Bolsheviks gained support by advocating an immediate end to the war and the handing over of land to the peasants.

The impact of the Bolsheviks was demonstrated in July 1917, during what was known as the "July Days". Sailors from the naval base of Kronstadt joined soldiers and workers in Petrograd and demanded that the Petrograd Soviet assume power. The leaders refused to do so. Some historians think that the Bolsheviks had a real chance to take power themselves during these days: all they needed to do was lead the demonstrators and take over in the name of the Soviet. The "July Days" proved how weak the Provisional Government was and how important the Bolsheviks were becoming.

By November 1917 the Bolsheviks were so strong that they were able to lead the Bolshevik "October Revolution", after which the first Bolshevik government, known as the *Sovnarkom*, was set up.

| Provisional Government | Petrograd Soviet |
|---|---|
| Wished to continue war against Germany and Austria | Wished to bring First World War to an end by means of a peace treaty, but in the meanwhile saw need to defend Russia (which, in effect, meant continuing the war) |
| Would not agree to peasants' seizure of land, but agreed that a future parliament (constituent assembly) would resolve the problem | Would not agree to the peasants' seizure of land, but promised that a future parliament (constituent assembly) would hand over the land to the peasants |

◁ 1  At the First All-Russian Congress of Soviets, June 1917: a painting by P. Vasilyev. That Stalin is facing in the same direction as Lenin, who addresses the audience, seems to reflect the way in which Stalin sided with Lenin on almost every issue. Stalin was to become the apostle of Lenin after the latter's death in 1924.

Stalin worked behind the scenes between the two revolutions of 1917:

> The labouring masses of Petrograd knew Stalin but little at that time. He did not seek popularity. Lacking ability as a speaker, he avoided mass meetings. But not a single party conference, not a serious organizational meeting of any consequence, was held without Stalin addressing it. The active party members knew him well on account of that.

That was how Bazhanov, one of Stalin's secretaries, a peasant, described Stalin at least ten years later. Stalin apparently spoke little in public; he chose his words carefully, and revealed little of his true feelings. But his influence in the party was great.

## The Bolshevik "October Revolution"

Stalin considered that the Bolsheviks had taken a great risk by seizing power in November 1917, in the "October Revolution", but his confidence in Lenin and his support of him were firm. He wrote in an article:

> What did it mean to start a revolt at such a time? . . . It meant staking everything on one card. But Lenin was not afraid to take risks, for he knew — he perceived with his far-seeing eye — that a revolution was inevitable, that it would be victorious, that a revolt in Russia would pave the way for the end of the imperialist war [First World War], that it would stir the tortured masses of the West, that a revolt in Russia would turn the imperialist war into a civil war, that it would produce the Soviet republic, which would serve as a rampart for the revolutionary movement of the whole world.

The Bolsheviks became more and more excited by the idea that the revolution in Russia would prove to be a spark which would ignite the flame of revolution around the world. They foresaw that revolutions would take place everywhere, especially in the advanced industrial countries, such as Germany, Great Britain and France, and they felt that a new society based on freedom and democracy was about to emerge everywhere. Stalin, however, remained sober and careful amid this excitement. There were no grand speeches from him.

## Stalin the Bureaucrat
## Government Offices

By 1920 Stalin had accumulated many offices, as you can see from the Date List (pages 71-2). He was well qualified for the post of Chairman for Nationalities which he was given in the Sovnarkom, for he had been born a Georgian (Georgia was a *republic* in the Caucasus) and he had worked on the nationalities problem in 1912-13, under the guidance of Lenin. The post of Chairman for Nationalities was an important one. since about half the population of Soviet Russia were not Russians: there were Armenians, Ukrainians, Tatars, Uzbeks, Chuvash, Kazakhs, Azerbaidzhanis and so on.

"Stalin, who does not like to waste words" was the comment Pestkovsky, a Polish Bolshevik and Stalin's deputy in the People's Commissariat of Nationalities, added in his reminiscences to the following description of a conversation he had had with Stalin as Chairman for Nationalities:

> *Pestkovsky*: Comrade Stalin, are you the People's Commissar for Nationalities?
>
> *Stalin*: Yes.
>
> *Pestkovsky*: Have you offices for the commissariat?
>
> *Stalin*: No.
>
> *Pestkovsky*: Right then, I shall find some for you.
>
> *Stalin*: All right, what do you need?
>
> *Pestkovsky*: Nothing but credentials so that I may get help.
>
> *Stalin*: Very well.

2   Stalin in 1919, aged 39. Note the tunic which was his normal attire until the Great Fatherland War, when he donned military uniform.

## The Power of the Bolsheviks

Stalin, looking back on the tasks that the Bolshevik party (renamed the *Russian Communist Party (Bolsheviks)* in 1918) had faced after the "October Revolution", wrote in an article in 1918:

> The period 1917-18 was crucial for our party and our state. The party then first became the ruling power. For the first time in the history of humanity a new power arose, that of the soviets of workers and peasants. To transform our party, which had hitherto existed illegally, on to new rails, to create the organizational foundations of the new proletarian state, to find the forms for the relations between the party and the soviets, to ensure the leadership of the party and the normal development of the soviets – all of these constituted the most complex organizational problem facing our party.

It is apparent from these words that the power which had been handed to the soviets in November 1917 had, in fact, passed to the Russian Communist Party by 1918. In this case, the men at the top of the RCP were obviously in a very powerful position. Stalin was among them. He was Lenin's right-hand man, as Pestkovsky also wrote in his reminiscences:

> Lenin could not get along without Stalin for a single day . . . . In the course of the day Lenin would telephone Stalin innumerable times or he would drop in and take Stalin with him. Stalin spent most of his time with Lenin. What he did there I do not know, but once, entering Lenin's office, I observed an interesting scene. On the wall was a large map of Russia. Two chairs were in front of it. On the chairs stood Lenin and Stalin and with their fingers they were tracing the northern boundary, I think, in the neighbourhood of Finland.

## Party Offices

Stalin built up his power and expanded his influence within the Russian Communist Party more than within the Government. At the time of the "October Revolution" in 1917 he was already a member of the Central Committee (CC) of the RSDLP (as the RCP was then called). In 1919, because the CC had expanded, a Political Bureau – *Politburo* – consisting of the most important members of the CC was set up, and Stalin was elected a member of it. In March 1919 Stalin was elected a member of the Organizational Bureau – *Orgburo* – which involved him in a lot of office work which he enjoyed. Being in the Orgburo also made information about the party members available to him. One of his duties as member of the Orgburo was to find officials for important posts – people whom the Communist Party could trust. Stalin seized this opportunity to put people who supported him into these posts. In 1922 Stalin was elected *Secretary General* (the chief secretary) of the Central Committee, but this did not yet make him head of the party, since Lenin was still alive.

## Offices held by Stalin during the Civil War

The Civil War between the Bolshevik *Red Army* and the anti-revolutionary, anti-Bolshevik *White Army* lasted from June 1918 until December 1920. Although Trotsky, as Commissar for War, was supposed to be superior to Stalin, Stalin still played a key role during the war.

In May 1918 Stalin had been given the job of making sure that food supplies were transported to northern Russia (this included Moscow and Petrograd) from the north Caucasus, a rich grain-producing area. Northern Russia could not survive without importing grain in this way. It was vital that the

3   Another painting by Vasilyev, showing the close ▷
relationship between Lenin and Stalin.

Red Army in Moscow got enough food during the Civil War, so that they could defend the territory they held against the Whites.

In June 1918 Stalin went to Tsaritsyn* to organize the despatching of grain from there to Moscow. He arrived with a 450-man guard, because it was a White area. He wrote to Lenin from Tsaritsyn on 7 July 1918:

> I am driving and bullying all those who require it. You can rest assured that we shall spare nobody, ourselves or others, and the grain will be obtained.

*Renamed Stalingrad in 1925, and now known as Volgograd.

It was. Grain intended for the city of Baku on the Caspian Sea was seized by some of Stalin's men from the man who was guarding it. They justified themselves for taking it by saying to him: "If we do not get grain, and go back to Stalin with empty hands, we shall be shot." The man went to see Stalin and pleaded that the grain should go to the starving people of Baku. Stalin rejected the plea:

> What nonsense you are talking. If we lose Baku, it is nothing. We shall take it again within a few months or a year at the most. If we lose Moscow, we lose everything. Then the revolution is over.

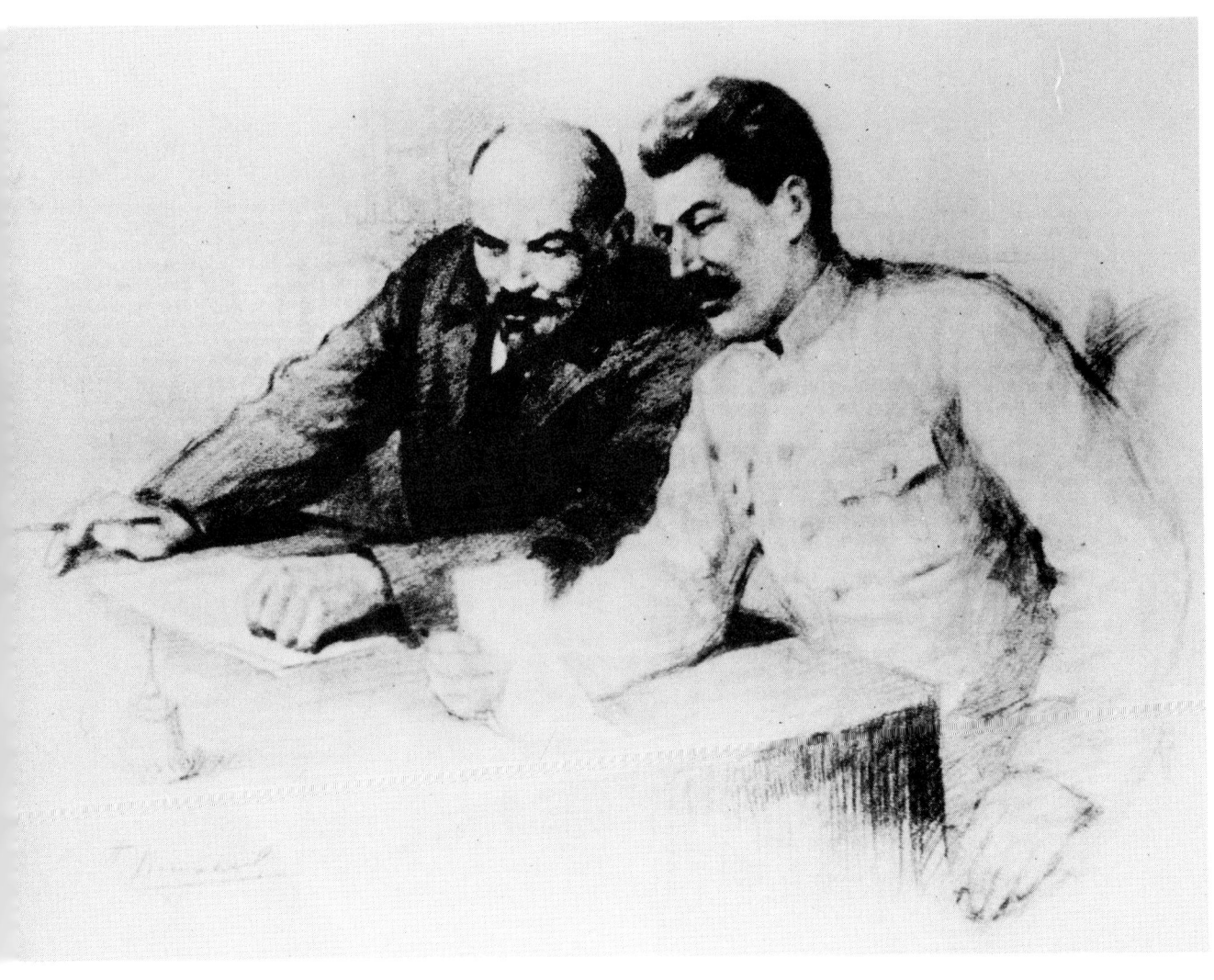

4   Delegates to the 8th Congress of the Russian Communist Party (Bolsheviks), March 1919. Lenin sits in the centre, with Stalin on his right and Kalinin on his left.

5   Famine affected Soviet Russia between 1918 and 1922. The suffering was worst in 1921 and 1922 due to the ravages of the Civil War. This picture shows a camp at Samara on the Volga in 1921.

One of the men involved related the incident to an American journalist several years later. The grain was sent to Moscow.

## Stalin and Trotsky

Some Red Army officers in Tsaritsyn were refusing to obey the orders given to them by the generals and military experts whom Trotsky had placed at the head of the Red Army. Stalin sympathised with the rebellious officers while he was in Tsaritsyn. Trotsky was furious at Stalin's interference in the

military preparations for the defence of Tsaritsyn and sent a telegraph to Lenin on 4 October 1918:

> I insist categorically on Stalin's recall.
> Things are going badly on the Tsaritsyn
> front despite superabundance of military
> forces . . . . Tsaritsyn must either obey or
> get out of the way.

6   Those who died from hunger had to be collected ▷ in carts. This is 1922.

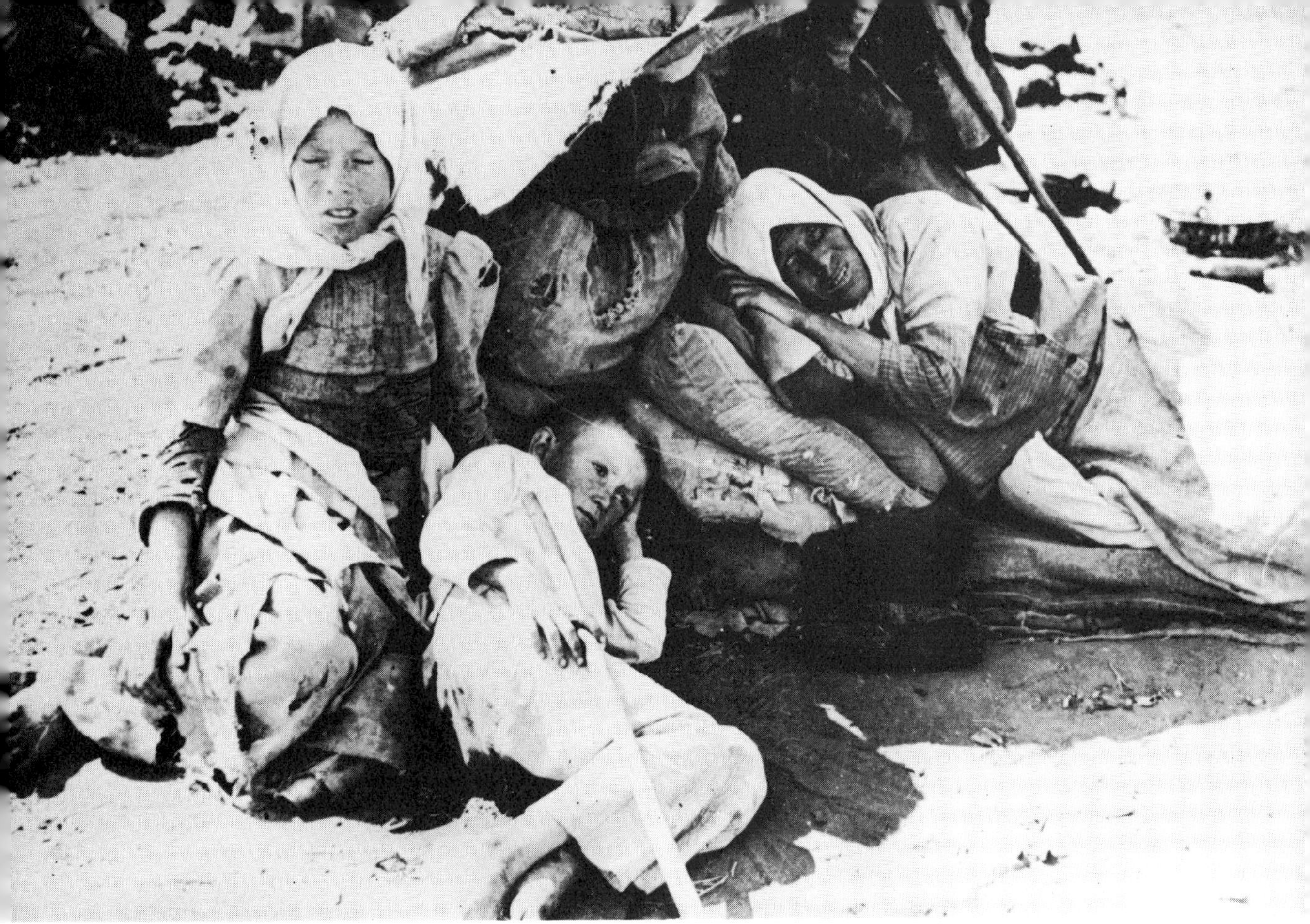

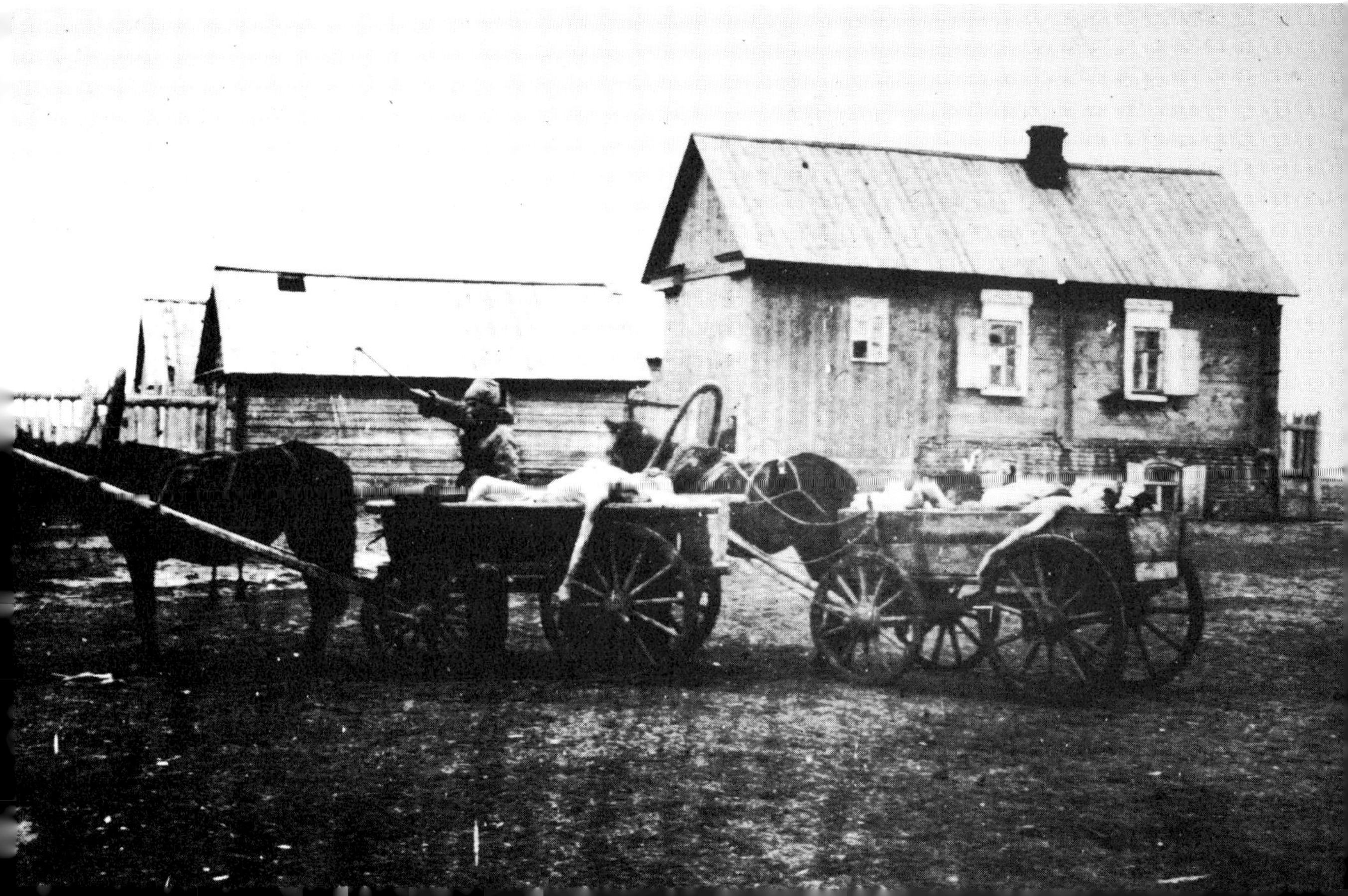

The following day Trotsky wrote again:

> . . . the activities of Stalin are wrecking all my plans.

Lenin immediately recalled Stalin.

Stalin returned to Tsaritsyn again, however, on 11 October and a few days later the White forces who had been besieging Tsaritsyn were finally repelled. The credit for the Red Army success was disputed between Stalin and Trotsky.

About a year later the Politburo decided to award Trotsky the *Order of the Red Banner*, in recognition of his successful defence of Petrograd against General Yudenich, the White Commander. Stalin was also awarded the Order of the Red Banner for his services in the defence of Petrograd and on the Southern Front. Bukharin said to Kalinin, who had apparently protested at Stalin's being awarded the Red Banner:

> Don't you understand? It is Lenin's idea. Stalin can't live unless he gets what someone else gets. He will never forget it.

This comment was recorded by Trotsky in his autobiography.

Stalin never forgave Trotsky for the insult of having him recalled from Tsaritsyn by Lenin. He took every opportunity of slighting him thereafter. Back in Moscow, Stalin worked at redeeming himself with Lenin and succeeded, for Lenin told Trotsky:

> Stalin is anxious to work on the Southern Front . . . . As for me, I think it is necessary to make every effort to arrange to work in conjunction with Stalin.

Lenin had a problem with Stalin who did not bother to send copies of some of his despatches to Trotsky, even though he was Commissar for War. Lenin usually forwarded to Trotsky any important messages which he had received from Stalin. And he once tried to solve the problem by sending the following note, bearing his own signature, to Trotsky, with the instruction that he should send it on to Stalin:

> Address all military communications to Trotsky as well, otherwise there may be a dangerous gap.

Lenin's idea was that Trotsky would see that he was ordering Stalin to send Trotsky his despatches. Stalin would not know, however, that Trotsky had seen the note.

## Humble or Arrogant?

Stalin had opponents other than Trotsky and enjoyed arguments. But if Lenin sided with an opponent of Stalin, Stalin always backed down, pretending to be modest and humble. On the other hand, he could be arrogant when he was sure of himself. In June 1919, after the Reds had captured the fort of Krasnaya Gorka on the Gulf of Finland, near Petrograd, Stalin sent the following telegram to Lenin:

> Naval experts say that the capture of Krasnaya Gorka from the sea is not possible according to naval science. I can only deplore such so-called science. The swift capture of Gorka was due to continual interference in the operations by me and by civilians generally, even to the point of overruling orders on land and sea and imposing our own.
>
> I consider it my duty to declare that I shall continue to act in this way in the future, despite all my respect for science.

Evidently Stalin's interference in military operations in Tsaritsyn had not been an isolated occurrence.

## After the Civil War

When the Civil War ended in December 1920 many people who had been fighting needed jobs in civilian life. Trotsky, writing years later in exile, described how the Red Army soldiers were given employment and formed the bureaucracy (civil service), which was run much in the same way as the army had been:

> The demobilization of five million Red Army men played no small part in the formation of the bureaucracy. The victorious commanders obtained leading posts in the local soviets, in the economy, in education and they persistently introduced that régime which had ensured victory in the civil war.

That "régime" was the non-democratic one by which the army commanders gave orders without discussing them beforehand and punished anyone who did not carry them out. These commanders then got the leading posts in the civil service and continued to give orders to the workers and peasants, treating them as if they were unruly soldiers who had to be disciplined and taught to be more efficient. The result of this, as Trotsky continued, was that

> on all sides the masses were cut off gradually from actual participation in the leadership of the country.

### Stalin and Lenin

In a moment of pleasure at one of Stalin's successes Lenin once referred to Stalin as the "wonderful Georgian". However, by

7  Lenin and his wife, Nadezhda Krupskaya, with their nephew Viktor and a worker's daughter Vera in Gorky, just outside Moscow. Lenin was convalescing there after a stroke.

1922 he began to have doubts. He knew that the Communist Party needed Stalin, but he was aware too that Stalin did not always carry out his instructions. Lenin saw by the end that Stalin was ambitious for power, and he also saw that a split was developing between Stalin and Trotsky, which would greatly harm the party. Lenin could work to prevent this split happening as long as he was in good health. Then from December 1921 Lenin was persistently ill and in May 1922 he suffered the first of three strokes, which left him paralyzed and unable to speak for a while. He dictated his fears about the rivalry of Stalin and Trotsky to his wife, Nadezhda Krupskaya.

## Disagreement over Georgia

A point over which Stalin and Lenin disagreed was whether Georgia should be made a part of the Russian Soviet Federative Socialist Republic (*RSFSR*), as the Russian part of the country was to be called when the Union of Soviet Socialist Republics (*USSR*) was founded in 1922, or whether Georgia should be a republic on its own. Lenin was in favour of Georgia's becoming a republic of the USSR, with a fair amount of freedom to decide its own policy. Stalin wanted Georgia to become a part of the RSFSR and to be ruled from Moscow.

Georgia was Stalin's native area, but he did not like to call himself a Georgian: he identified closely with the Russians, calling himself a "Muscovite" (a native of Moscow) and writing of "We Russian Bolsheviks" and "We Russian Marxists". He had learnt to speak Russian very well but his Georgian accent was noticeable. He wanted Georgia to be tied closely to Moscow. One idea Stalin had was that Georgia should form a Federation with Armenia and Azerbaidzhan. The Communist Party in Georgia was unhappy at this idea and appealed to Lenin for his support. The Communist Party in Georgia then applied formally to become a republic

of the Soviet Union. Stalin was furious, accusing Georgian communists of being Georgian nationalists. Stalin's struggle with the Communist Party in Georgia was very heated, and on one occasion one of Stalin's supporters there, Ordzhonikidze, struck one of the Georgian communists. Lenin, hearing of this, could not forgive the action. He dictated the following to his private secretary, Fotieva, from his sick-bed:

If matters have come to such a pass that Ordzhonikidze could go to the extreme of applying physical violence . . . we can imagine what a mess we have got ourselves into.

It is quite natural that in such circumstances the "freedom to secede from the union" [the right of Georgia to become independent of Soviet Russia] by which we justify ourselves will be a mere scrap of paper, unable to defend the non-Russian from the onslaught of that really Russian man, the Great Russian chauvinist, in substance a rascal and a tyrant, such as the typical Russian bureaucrat is. There is no doubt that the minute percentage of Soviet and sovietized workers will drown in that tide of chauvinistic Great Russian riffraff like a fly in milk.

I think that Stalin's haste and infatuation with pure administration, together with his spite against "social nationalism", played a fatal role here. In politics spite generally plays the basest of roles.

Fotieva told Trotsky that Lenin had seen through Stalin and wished to come out against him openly, in front of the whole party. Lenin, he said, was "preparing a bomb" (sensation). With this information, Trotsky could have secured a political advantage over Stalin by attacking him in the Politburo, knowing that Lenin would agree. However, Trotsky did not take this opportunity. He merely stated in public that Stalin had made a bad mistake over Georgia, which became a republic, as Lenin had wished. Stalin replied in a speech denying that he had had any disagreement with Lenin:

> This is untrue, comrades. That is gossip. I have never had any disagreements with the party or with Lenin on the national question. Trotsky must be referring to one insignificant incident that took place when comrade Lenin before the Twelfth *Congress* of our party [1923] reproached me for following too strict an organizational policy towards the Georgian semi-nationalists, semi-communists . . . saying that I was persecuting them. Subsequent facts showed, however, that the so-called deviationists deserved still more severe treatment than I . . . gave them. Lenin did not and could not know these facts because he was ill and not in a position to follow events.

Lenin did know all about it though. On 4 January 1923 he dictated a postscript to the document which became known after his death as his "Testament". He now recommended that Stalin be removed from the post of Secretary General of the Communist Party:

> Stalin is too rude and this defect, although quite tolerable in our midst and in relations among us communists, becomes intolerable in the post of Secretary General. This is why I suggest that comrades think of a way of removing Stalin from that post and appointing another man to replace him who in all other respects differs from comrade Stalin in having only one advantage, namely, that of being tolerant, more loyal, more polite, and more considerate to his comrades, less capricious, etc.

Having further cause to complain of Stalin's behaviour, Lenin wrote to him in March 1923:

> Respected Comrade Stalin,
>     You were rude enough to call my wife to the telephone and give her a dressing down. Although she expressed the willingness to forget what you said, this fact, nevertheless, became known, through her, to Zinoviev and Kamenev. I do not intend to forget so easily what was done against me, and there is no need to point out that what is done against my wife I consider to be done against me also. Therefore I ask you to consider whether you agree to take back what you said and apologize, or whether you prefer to break off relations between us.
>     With respects,
>     Lenin

### Lenin's death saves Stalin

Lenin died on 21 January 1924. Between then and the 13th Party Congress held from 23-31 May 1924 the Communist Party launched a membership drive among the "workers from the bench" and the existing membership was *purged*. Stalin was able to ensure that newly recruited members would accept the authority of the party leaders.

On the eve of the 13th Party Congress Lenin's wife sent the document which he had dictated from his sickbed to the Politburo. She said that it had been Lenin's wish that the document (now referred to as his "Testament") should be submitted to the Party Congress. The Central Committee of the Communist Party met to decide whether this wish should be carried out. One of Stalin's secretaries, Bazhanov later described how Stalin seemed to be aware that his fate was being decided at this meeting:

> Painful embarrassment paralyzed the whole gathering. Stalin . . . felt small and miserable. Despite self-control and forced calm one could clearly read on his face that his fate was being decided.

Zinoviev spoke up for Stalin:

> Comrades, the last will, every word of Vladimir Ilich Lenin is undoubtedly to

be regarded by us as law . . . . On one point, however, we are fortunate to be able to report that Ilich's fears have not been confirmed. I refer to the point concerning our Secretary General. You have all been witnesses to our work together over the past few months.

Stalin was off the hook. Did he feel obliged to Zinoviev and Kamenev and the others who had saved his career? Not at all. We shall see how he rewarded them — with death.

8   Gregory Evseevich Zinoviev.

# Chapter Two 1924-1929

# Stalin the Apostle of Lenin, and Stalin's Struggle with his Rivals

## In Memory of Lenin

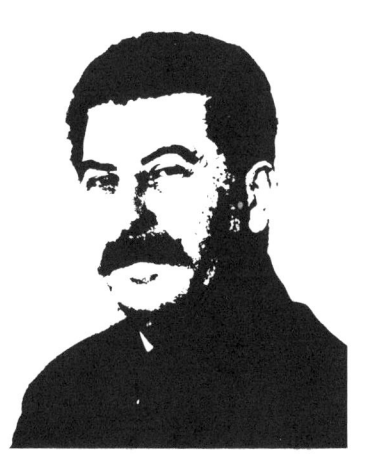

With Lenin dead, an extraordinary thought took root in the minds of some of the Russian Communist Party (Bolsheviks): do not bury Lenin, but mummify his body — just like some Pharoah of old — and keep it in a

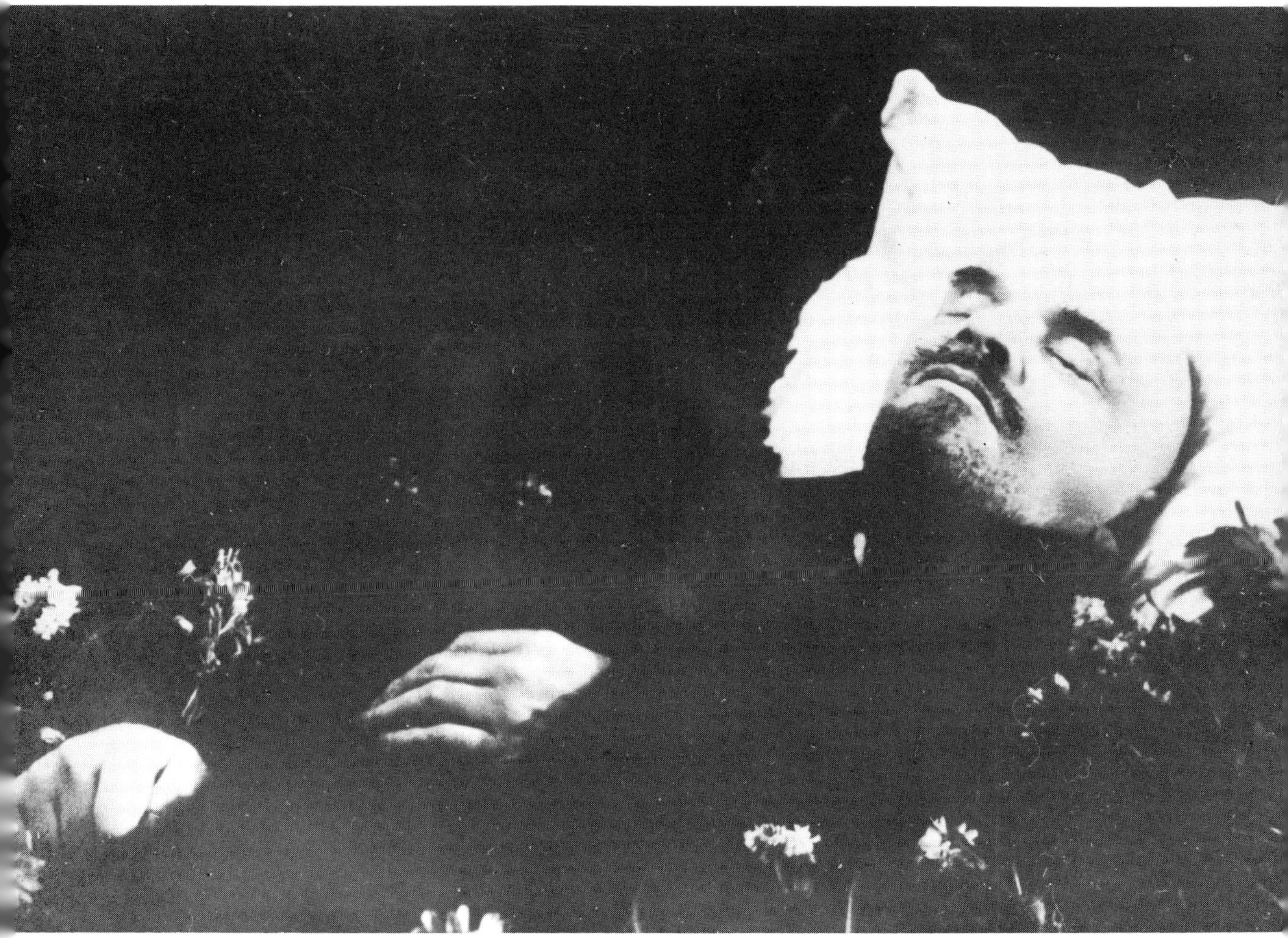

9 Lenin in his coffin, Gorky, outside Moscow, 1924.

mausoleum where everyone could come to see it. This was done, and since 1924 millions of people have been to Moscow to see Lenin. The mausoleum is so sacred that photography is forbidden inside it, and no one may even stop and stare; you must keep moving when in the tomb. How Lenin would have hated it all if he were still alive! On 30 January 1924 a letter from Lenin's wife, Krupskaya, appeared in the party newspaper *Pravda*. In it she pleaded against the whole idea of putting up memorials to Lenin:

> I have a serious request to make: do not allow your mourning for Ilich [Lenin] to take the form of external reverence for his person. Do not put up memorials to him, do not name palaces after him, do not hold festivals to commemorate him — he attached so little importance to all this when he was alive, all this was a burden to him.

However, the plea was not heeded: the city of Petrograd was renamed Leningrad and Lenin's body was preserved and put on display, as Stalin wished. Stalin wanted to proclaim himself the chief apostle of the great dead leader Lenin: he saw that people's veneration for the great dead leader would be encouraged and increased if they were able to see his body in a sacred atmosphere; and if people's veneration of the great dead leader grew, so also would their veneration of his apostle, Stalin.

**Stalin the Apostle of Lenin**

On 26 January Stalin made the following remarkable speech to the 2nd All-Union Congress of Soviets:

> Comrades! We communists are people of a special mould. We are made of special stuff. We are they who form the army of the great proletarian general, the army of comrade Lenin. There is nothing above the privilege of belonging to this army. There is nothing higher than the calling of a mem-

ber of the party whose founder and leader is comrade Lenin. It is not given to every man to endure the tribulations and trials which go with membership of such a party. Sons of the working class, sons of need and strife, sons of unequalled privations and heroic strivings — such are the men, who, first and foremost, are fitted to be members of such a party. That is why the party of Leninists, the party of communists, is also called the party of the working class.

The party of the working class was thus reminded of how special it was: its members were privileged, chosen people. As such, they had special duties which Stalin listed for them, like biblical commandments:

> Leaving us, comrade Lenin bequeathed to us the duty of holding high and keeping pure the great calling of members of the party.
> We swear to thee, comrade Lenin, that we shall fulfil this thy commandment with honour.
> Leaving us, comrade Lenin bequeathed to us the duty of regarding the unity of the party as the apple of our eye.
> We swear to thee, comrade Lenin, that we shall fulfil this thy commandment with honour.
> Leaving us, comrade Lenin bequeathed to us the duty of keeping and strengthening the dictatorship of the proletariat.
> We swear to thee, comrade Lenin, that, not sparing our strength, we shall fulfil this thy commandment with honour.
> Leaving us, comrade Lenin bequeathed to us the duty of strengthening with all our might the union of workers and peasants.
> We swear to thee, comrade Lenin, that we shall fulfil this thy commandment with honour.
> Leaving us, comrade Lenin bequeathed to us the duty of strengthening and extending the union of republics.

We swear to thee, comrade Lenin, that we shall fulfil this thy commandment with honour.

Leaving us, comrade Lenin bequeathed to us the duty of being loyal to the principles of the Communist International.

We swear to thee, comrade Lenin, that, not sparing our lives, we shall strengthen and extend the union of the toilers of the whole world — the Communist International.

These duties, which Stalin said Lenin had left to the party, were the party's creed of beliefs and aims. Lenin died and Leninism (the creed he left) was born. How faithful Stalin was to the "creed", when he was doing battle with his opponents in the party, will be seen later in this chapter.

Stalin was not the only one to speak of Leninism. Zinoviev, also, for example, had the idea of becoming an apostle of Lenin. He was communist party leader in Leningrad and Chairman of the *Comintern*. In an article in *Pravda* on 30 January 1924 he wrote:

Lenin is dead. Leninism lives. It lives in our great party, in the Communist International, in the revolutionary movement of the whole world. When the proletarian revolution is victorious throughout the world that will be first and foremost the victory of Lenin.

Stalin too had said, in his speech about the duties left to the party by the dead leader, that they would be prepared to die in their fight to spread the victory of the revolution all over the world. Did he totally keep this promise?

In *The Foundations of Leninism* (a collection of lectures given at the Sverdlov University in Moscow, and later published) Stalin said with insistence that Leninism meant working for the victory of the proletarian revolution right across the world, now that it had triumphed in Russia:

And so, what is Leninism?

Some say that Leninism is the application of *Marxism* to the particular conditions of the situation in Russia . . . . We know, however, that Leninism is not merely a Russian but an international phenomenon rooted in the whole of international development . . . .

Leninism is Marxism of the era of imperialism and of the proletarian revolution. To be more exact, Leninism is the theory and tactics of the dictatorship of the proletariat in particular. Marx and Engels pursued their activities in the pre-revolutionary period (we have the proletarian revolution in mind), when developed imperialism did not yet exist, in the period of the proletarians' preparation for revolution, in the period when the proletarian revolution was not yet an immediate practical inevitability. Lenin, however, the disciple of Marx and Engels, pursued his activities in the period of developed imperialism, in the period of the unfolding proletarian revolution, when the proletarian revolution had already triumphed in one country, had smashed bourgeois democracy and had ushered in the era of proletarian democracy, the era of the soviets. That is why Leninism is the further development of Marxism.

Also in *The Foundations of Leninism* we find Stalin's definition of the role of the party:

The party must be, first of all, the vanguard [leader] of the working class.

The party is not only the vanguard detachment of the working class. If it desires really to direct the struggle of the class it must at the same time be the organised detachment of its class. The party is the highest form of class association of the proletarians, whose political leadership must extend to every other form of organization of the proletariat.

The party is the highest form of organization of the proletariat. The party is the principle guiding force within the class of proletarians and among the organizations of that class.

The proletariat needs the party for the purpose of achieving and maintaining its dictatorship. The party is an instrument of the dictatorship of the proletariat.

Stalin repeats over and over again how the working class can maintain the power it gained by the revolution only by accepting the organization and the leadership of the party.

Stalin then described how party and state work should be carried out:

Leninist style has two specific features: a) Russian revolutionary sweep and b) American efficiency. The style of Leninism is a combination of these two specific features in party and state work.

As the apostle of Lenin, Stalin always spoke as if Lenin's writings were above criticism. If someone's point of view could be supported by a quotation from Lenin's collected works (over 50 volumes), then that point of view was correct. If somebody failed to present Lenin as a tremendous genius in a piece of writing, then that writing was false.

For example, in October 1924 Trotsky published a volume of speeches and writings on the "October Revolution". In his introduction, "Lessons of October", he did not present Lenin, in the opinion of Stalin and his followers, as a great enough genius. Bukharin, an opponent of Trotsky, wrote:

There is Trotsky. Lenin is visible in the distance and there is some sort of . . . Central Committee. Is this the way for Marxists to write history? It is a caricature of Marxism.

And Stalin also wrote in the press:

Trotsky has thus failed to present Lenin as he really was — the greatest Marxist of the present age. He has painted a portrait not of Lenin the giant but of some kind of . . . dwarf.

## The Campaign against Trotsky

In "Lessons of October" Trotsky also attacked Kamenev and Zinoviev for their part in the "October Revolution": they had been opposed to the Bolsheviks' seizure of power. Stalin sided with Kamenev and Zinoviev against Trotsky and used the issue of "Lessons of October" as a starting point for a political campaign against Trotsky. In the campaign Stalin attacked Trotsky with many of the harsh things which Lenin had written between 1904 and 1917 about Trotsky's theory of "permanent revolution". Stalin continually attacked Trotsky in the party, making him appear an *"oppositionist"* to the party line. This forced Trotsky to give up all his important government offices, and in January 1925 Trotsky resigned as Commissar for War. Stalin had successfully eliminated Trotsky as a rival for power within the party.

"Lessons of October" had given Stalin the opportunity to start a political campaign against Trotsky, but, as Zinoviev realized later on, if this opportunity had not arisen, Stalin would have found another. Trotsky recalled in his book *The Stalin School of Falsification* how he had asked Zinoviev whether the campaign against him would have happened if he had never written "Lessons of October". Zinoviev had replied:

Yes it would. "Lessons of October" merely served as a pretext. Failing that a different motive would have been found and the discussion would have assumed slightly different forms, nothing more . . . . You must understand that it was a struggle for power. The trick was to string together old disagreements with new issues. For this reason "Trotskyism" was born.

The "old disagreements" were the words of Lenin which Stalin "strung together"

10  Lev Davidovich Trotsky, the most formidable intellectual opponent of Stalin. However, Trotsky was a poor politician. He found it difficult to get on with people.

with the new issue of "Lessons of October", to attack his rival for power, Trotsky.

## Stalin against Kamenev and Zinoviev

Having eliminated Trotsky, in January 1925 Stalin broke with the triumvirate which he had formed with Kamenev and Zinoviev in the spring of 1923 to block Trotsky as Lenin's successor. Just as he had used the issue of "Lessons of October" as a starting point for his attack on Trotsky, so he now used the issue of "socialism in one country" as a starting point for an attack on Kamenev and Zinoviev. Stalin was changing sides in two ways: he was attacking people whom he had formerly supported; and he was supporting ideas which he had previously attacked. His aim was to eliminate his rivals for power. Because he was cunning enough to use vital issues over which there were genuine disagreements, people did not realize until later his true motive. Stalin was playing a dangerous game, but he was a brilliant political tactician!

Kamenev and Zinoviev supported Trotsky's idea of permanent revolution, which meant that socialism could only be built in the USSR if socialist revolutions had occurred in the advanced industrial countries first. Kamenev and Zinoviev attacked the idea that there could be "socialism in one country" (Soviet Russia), and Zinoviev called it "national narrow-mindedness". Stalin also had said, in *The Foundations of Leninism*, that "socialism in one country" was impossible. But now he changed his view, siding with Bukharin, Rykov and Tomsky to disagree with Kamenev and Zinoviev, and he now wrote in *The Problems of Leninism* that "socialism in one country" *was* possible. He argued that those who opposed his view that socialism could be built in Soviet Russia lacked faith in the revolution and that, worse, they were holding back the world socialist revolution by their doubts. Stalin sensed that in voicing this point of view he would be voicing the feelings of the majority of the party members, and he was confident therefore that from the beginning he would have more support than Kamenev and Zinoviev. Stalin had rightly sensed the feelings and attitude at the time of the party members: Alexander Barmine wrote in *One Who Survived* (published in New York in 1945):

> Our general mood was one of healthy optimism. We were sure of ourselves and the future. We believed that our socialist country would be able, within a few years, to offer the world an example of a society founded on principles of liberty and equality. This belief was shared by almost all of us.

In his biography of Stalin, Trotsky included the following comment about Stalin's ability to sense the common feeling, which he had made to a friend in 1924:

> The dialectics of history have already hooked him and will raise him up. He is needed by all of them — by the tired radicals, by the bureaucrats, by the *Nepmen* [traders], by the *kulaks* [rich peasants], by the upstarts, by the sneaks, by all the worms that are crawling out of the upturned soil of the manured revolution. He knows how to meet them on their own ground, he speaks their language and he knows how to lead them. He has the deserved reputation of an old revolutionary, which makes him invaluable to them as a blinker on the eyes of the country . . . .
> Of course, great developments in Europe, in Asia and in our country may intervene and upset all the speculations. But if everything continues to go automatically as it is going now, Stalin will just as automatically become dictator.

And there was nothing that Trotsky could do to stop him.

Having begun his campaign against Kamenev and Zinoviev over the issue of "socialism in one country", Stalin opposed them on other issues. Trotsky, Kamenev and Zinoviev favoured rapid industrialization, paid for partly by higher taxes on the kulaks (rich peasants) and partly by higher industrial prices. Against this Stalin, with Bukharin, Rykov and Tomsky, wanted an alliance between the industrial workers and the peasants, and attacked those who wished to eliminate the kulaks. Kamenev and Zinoviev said that the kulaks were a political and economic danger. Stalin said they presented no political danger. He also supported individual peasant private farming. Having stood up for Kamenev and Zinoviev when Trotsky had attacked their role in the "October Revolution", Stalin now attacked them himself for their behaviour in the revolution.

The result of Stalin's attacking Kamenev and Zinoviev on all these issues was that they were all expelled from the Politburo for being "Left" oppositionists: Zinoviev in July 1926 and Kamenev and Trotsky in October 1926. Stalin had thus eliminated Trotsky, Kamenev and Zinoviev as rivals for power within the party.

## Stalin against Bukharin, Rykov and Tomsky

Having eliminated Kamenev and Zinoviev, the "Left" opposition, by siding with Bukharin, Rykov and Tomsky against them, Stalin in 1928 turned again, to attack Bukharin, Rykov and Tomsky, the "Right" opposition.

The "Right" point of view supported by Bukharin, Rykov and Tomsky was the one which Stalin had supported between 1925-27: that the kulaks were not a political danger, and there was no need to eliminate them; that individual peasant private farming should continue; and that Soviet Russia should industrialize slowly, etc. In December 1925 in a speech to the 14th Congress of the Russian Communist Party (Bolsheviks) Stalin had criticized the attitude of those communists who wanted to destroy the kulaks:

If you were to ask communists which the

party is better prepared for — to strip the kulak or, instead, to enter into an alliance with the middle peasant (those just able to make a living) — I think that ninety-nine out of a hundred would say that the party was best prepared for the slogan, "Beat the kulak". Just say the word and they will strip the kulak.

But in 1928 he began to praise that attitude. Stalin now said that individual peasant private farming must be replaced by *collective* farming, and that industrialization must take place rapidly. He called for even faster growth rates in industry than the "Left" opposition, which he had opposed, had asked for earlier. In October 1928 the first *Five Year Plan* was introduced and collectivization began (see Chapter 3).

The result of Stalin's attacking the points of view of Bukharin, Tomsky and Rykov was that Bukharin and Rykov were expelled from the Politburo — Bukharin in November 1929 and Rykov in December 1930. Tomsky was not expelled, but in July 1930 he was not re-elected to the Politburo.

And so Stalin had eliminated all his rivals for power within the party. Some time later, Bukharin, when he was in Paris in 1936, spoke of Stalin to Fyodor Dan (a Menshevik who had been deported from Soviet Russia in 1922 and who lived abroad for the rest of his life):

He [Stalin] is unhappy at not being able to convince everyone, himself included, that he is greater than everyone else; and this unhappiness of his may be his most human trait, perhaps the only human trait in him. But what is not human, but something diabolical, is that because of this unhappiness he cannot avoid taking revenge on people, on all people but especially on those who are in some way higher or better than he. If someone speaks better than he does, that man is for it! Stalin will not let him live, because that man is a constant reminder that he, Stalin, is not the first

and the best. If someone writes better, woe betide him because he, Stalin, has to be the best Russian writer. Marx, of course, no longer has anything to fear from him, except possibly to appear small to the Russian worker in comparison with the great Stalin. No, no Fyodor, he is a narrow-minded, malicious man — no, not a man, but a devil.

History was to show that Bukharin was right. Stalin did not love himself enough.

11   This cartoon from an émigré journal published in Paris shows a meeting of the Supreme Soviet (the Soviet parliament), where every member is Stalin. Bukharin remarked that "Stalin can't live unless he gets what someone else gets". (See page 16.)

# Chapter Three   The 1930s

# Stalin Supreme - Industrialization and Collectivization, and the Purges

Stalin could afford to spend his time in the mid-1920s doing battle with his political opponents as at that time there were no major problems to deal with in the Soviet Union. The country was back in the same good economic position that Imperial Russia had been in in 1913, just before the First World War. And there was no threat of invasion from abroad.

## New Problems
## The Threat of War

However, by 1927 Stalin believed or said he believed that the Soviet Union was facing the threat of war. In an article in *Pravda* on 28 July 1927 he wrote:

> Another imperialist war is unquestionably on the horizon. We refer not to some indefinite, vague "danger" of a new war but to the real and imminent threat of a new war in general, and of a war against the Soviet Union in particular . . . . England prefers wars fought by others . . . . Now and then she actually finds fools to pull her chestnuts out of the fire. The entire international situation, all the British government's operations against the Soviet Union — it holds secret conferences with the Powers on a policy against the Soviet Union, it subsidizes the "émigré" governments of the Ukraine, Georgia, Azerbaid-

zhan, Armenia, etc so as to instigate revolts in those republics of the Soviet Union, it finances groups of spies and terrorists to blow up bridges, set factories on fire, and terrorize Soviet legations abroad — all this undoubtedly proves that the British Tory government has definitely and resolutely undertaken to start a war against the Soviet Union.

The "émigré" governments whom Stalin here accused the British Government of supporting were the former, non-communist governments of the Ukraine, Georgia, Azerbaidzhan, etc, who had been sent into exile.

## Poor relations with China

Also in 1927, the Russians were upset by the actions of the Kuomintang, the revolutionary movement which ruled China. In 1923, when the Kuomintang had been led by Sun Yat-sen, China and the Soviet Union had signed a Sino-Soviet Treaty, under which the Soviet Union undertook to help the Kuomintang to unite China and said it would not try to impose communism on the country. China then welcomed Soviet political and military advice. But in 1927, under its new leader Chiang Kai-shek, the Kuomintang began to kill communists in China, and at the end of the year relations between China and

△

12    Stalin in 1930. Now the master, he looks every inch the leader. Even though the Soviet Union was at peace, Stalin is wearing semi-military uniform. This was due in part to the lasting impact of the Civil War on Soviet development.

the Soviet government were severed.

## Fading possibility of revolution spreading

The prospects of further revolutions occurring in Europe were receding. The mid-1920s were a prosperous time for Europe and, as is usually true, people were not interested in revolution when their country was in a sound economic position. The Soviet government felt discouraged.

## Peasants withhold grain

To add to the Soviet Union's problems, the government was not able to buy enough grain from the peasants in 1927-28 to feed the cities and the Red Army. The grain was available, but the peasants refused to sell it to the government because they thought the prices the government offered for it were too low. There was a simple remedy: increase prices, and the peasants would sell more. However, Stalin did not want to be dictated to by the peasants: he wanted to dictate to them. In a major party speech in 1928 Stalin announced his view of the situation: the problem was that the government had to rely on private producers of grain for food; the solution was therefore to get rid of the private producers, by replacing farming by private individuals with farming by collectives; modernize and socialize agriculture so that it matched Soviet industry:

The only way out of the situation is to overcome the capitalist elements in the village. We must not too long base Soviet power and the socialist structure on two different foundations: on the foundation of the largest and most unified socialist industry and on the foundation of the most divided and backward small peasant farming. It is necessary, gradually and resolutely, to re-fashion agriculture on a new technical basis, on the basis of large-scale production, pulling it up to socialist industry. Either we solve this problem and then final victory is guaranteed or we

13 Agriculture as it was before Stalin's scheme for mechanization. The farmer is sowing grain by hand and the horses behind are pulling a wooden harrow to cover the seed with earth.

△
14  Agriculture as it was to be: the tractor, the mechanical horse, could perform much more during a day than any living horse. It could pull machines which could sow, harrow, reap and so on. The tractor is the key to modern agriculture. The man in the centre is Leonid Alyamovsky, who conducted the first courses for tractor drivers in the Byelorussian Republic.

retreat from it without solving it and then the return to capitalism may become an inevitable development.

Note Stalin's concern about the victory of socialism.

◁ 15  Stalin, the leader, pointing the way ahead. He was not a very good public speaker. This portrait is posed and therefore untypical.

## Mechanization of Agriculture and Industrialization

The decision to modernize and mechanize agriculture and the belief that war was imminent affected the development of industry in the Soviet Union too. Heavy industry (metallurgical and machine-building industries) was made the centre of the Five Year Plan (1928-32). The Soviet Union was not to concentrate on producing consumer goods, like shoes, for example, of which any number produced would gradually run out as people bought and used them. Soviet industry was to produce machinery, machines that would in turn produce more machines: so that the number of products was constantly multiplying itself.

The centre of industrialization, the corner-stone, lies in the development of fuel resources, metallurgical production, finally in the development of machinery and tools for production. Either we achieve this or we shall be wiped out.

## The Victory of Socialism

Stalin was anxious that the Soviet Union should be able to defend itself from attack by other countries in the event of war. He was also anxious to prevent socialism in the Soviet Union from being "wiped out" by the capitalism of other countries.

> Our country is encircled . . . by capitalism. It is impossible to preserve our independence without having an adequately industrialized base for defence. It is impossible to create such an industrial base without mastering higher technology. This is what we need and that is what dictates to us the rapid tempo of industrialization.

Mechanization and socialization of agriculture and the development of heavy industry would go towards ensuring the "victory of socialism", which was Stalin's main aim, but he insisted that something else was also essential:

> To overthrow the power of the bourgeoisie and to set up the power of the proletariat in one country does not mean the safe-guarding of the final victory of socialism. After consolidating its power and leading the peasantry, the working class of a victorious country can and must build a socialist society. But does that mean that it can achieve the complete, final victory of socialism? Does it mean that it is able by its own efforts to consolidate full socialism and safeguard the country against intervention and therefore against the restoration of capitalism? No, it does not mean that. To ensure this it is necessary that the revolution be victorious in some other countries. Therefore it is an essen-tial task of our victorious revolution to further and aid revolution in other countries. Therefore a victorious revolution in one country must be seen, not as a self-sufficient force, but as a prop, a medium for the speeding up of the victory of the prole-tariat in other countries.

Stalin in 1928 was saying that the Russian revolution was a spark which should be made to ignite the flame of revolution in other countries.

## Collectivization

Stalin sought the victory of socialism. The interests of the state took precedence over the interests of any individual. All middle and poor peasants were put into collectives (kolkhozes) and all the better-off peasants, known as kulaks, were removed from the countryside. Over 5 million persons were deported to the far north and to the semi-deserts of Kazakhstan. Anyone who opposed these measures taken to socialize agriculture had also to be removed. In a speech to party activists on 13 April 1928 (which was typical of many of Stalin's speeches in 1928) Stalin was brutally frank about the need to wipe out all opponents of collectivization:

> Our policy is a class policy. He who thinks that one can conduct in the countryside a policy which will please everyone, the rich as well as the poor, is not a Marxist but an idiot, because, comrades, such a policy does not exist in the natural order of things.

"Class policy" was to wipe out the kulaks (the "richer peasants", although anyone who opposed collectivization was called a

16 Again a pose. Stalin is gazing into the future with great self-confidence. He is sure that the Soviet Union can build socialism (a highly developed indus-trial economy and a very productive agriculture) by itself.

"kulak") economically and politically, and often physically. Stalin showed little concern whether the kulaks he "removed" lived or died: in a 1929 speech he said:

> Now we are able to conduct a determined offensive against the kulaks, eliminating them as a class. Now liquidating the kulaks is being carried out by the masses of poor and middle peasants themselves. Now it is an integral part of the formation and development of collective farms. Hence it is ridiculous and foolish to talk at length about liquidating the kulaks. When the head is off, one does not mourn for the hair. There is another question no less ridiculous: whether kulaks should be permitted to join collective farms. Of course not, for they are the sworn enemies of collectivization.

The peasants' reaction to collectivization has been described by the famous Russian novelist Mikhail Sholokhov in *Virgin Soil Upturned:*

> Animals were slaughtered every night. Hardly had dusk fallen than the muffled bleats of sheep, the death squeals of pigs or the lowing of calves could be heard. Both those who had joined the collective farm and individual farmers slaughtered their stock. "Slaughter, they'll take it for meat anyway . . . . Slaughter, you won't

17  Mikhail Sholokhov reads from another of his novels, *And Quiet Flows the Don*, to a workers' club at the Krasny Bogatyr factory in 1929.

get meat on the collective farm . . . ,"
crept the insidious rumours. And they
slaughtered. They ate till they could eat
no more. Young and old suffered from
indigestion. At dinner-time tables groaned
under boiled and roasted meat. At dinner-
time everyone had a greasy mouth, everyone hiccoughed as if at a wake. Everyone
blinked like an owl, as if drunk from
eating.

If peasants showed themselves unwilling to
join a collective, the army was sent. However, not every soldier was willing to shoot
peasants. "I won't go," shouts a soldier in
the same novel, as preparations are being
made to go to a rich peasant's house — a
man with eleven children. "I won't go. I
don't know how to fight children . . . . For
God's sake!"

By 1936 most peasant farms had been
collectivized:

*Peasant households collectivized*
(Percentage)

| 1930 | 1931 | 1932 | 1933 | 1934 | 1935 | 1936 |
|------|------|------|------|------|------|------|
| 23.6 | 52.7 | 61.5 | 64.4 | 71.4 | 83.2 | 89.6 |

*Crop area collectivized*
(Percentage)

| 1930 | 1931 | 1932 | 1933 | 1934 | 1935 |
|------|------|------|------|------|------|
| 33.6 | 67.8 | 77.6 | 83.1 | 87.4 | 94.1 |

## Results of collectivization

One of the reasons for collectivization had
been to secure guaranteed supplies of grain
for the cities and the Red Army. How successful was the government in purchasing grain
from the collective farms?

*State purchases of grain*
(Millions of tonnes)

| 1928 | 1929 | 1930 | 1931 | 1932 | 1933 |
|------|------|------|------|------|------|
| 10.8 | 16.1 | 22.1 | 22.8 | 18.5 | 22.6 |

*Exports of grain*
(Millions of tonnes)

| 1927-28 | 1929 | 1930 | 1931 | 1932 | 1933 |
|---------|------|------|------|------|------|
| 0.03 | 0.18 | 4.76 | 5.06 | 1.73 | 1.69 |

These figures show the serious situation in
1932-33 when there was famine in parts of
the country. It was a man-made famine due
to too rapid collectivization. Millions of
people died but no mention of this was ever
made in the Soviet press.

By 1935 it was clear that collectivization
had not brought the rapid increase in agricultural production which Stalin had hoped
for. The agricultural production figures, in
the bottom table, went down in many cases.

*Agricultural Production*

|  | 1928 | 1929 | 1930 | 1931 | 1932 | 1933 | 1934 | 1935 |
|--|------|------|------|------|------|------|------|------|
| Grain harvest (Millions of tonnes) | 73.3 | 71.7 | 83.5 | 69.5 | 69.6 | 68.4 | 67.6 | 75.0 |
| Cattle (Million head) | 70.5 | 67.1 | 52.5 | 47.9 | 40.7 | 38.4 | 42.4 | 49.3 |
| Pigs | 26.0 | 20.4 | 13.6 | 14.4 | 11.6 | 12.1 | 17.4 | 22.6 |
| Sheep and goats | 146.7 | 147.0 | 108.8 | 77.7 | 52.1 | 50.2 | 51.9 | 61.1 |

Was the Soviet Union asking too much of its workers and collective farm peasants and expecting industrial and agricultural production to grow too rapidly? In a speech to the first All-Union *Conference* of Workers in Socialist Industry in Moscow in February 1931 Stalin gave this answer:

It is sometimes asked whether it is not possible to slow down the tempo a little. No, comrades, it is not possible. The tempo must not be reduced. On the contrary, we must increase it as much as is within our powers and capacities. This is dictated to us by our obligations to the workers and peasants of the Soviet Union. This is dictated to us by our obligations to the working class of the whole world.

To slow down the tempo would mean falling behind. And those who fall behind get beaten. But we do not want to be beaten. No, we refuse to be beaten. One aspect of the history of old Russia was the repeated beatings she suffered for falling behind, for her backwardness. She was beaten by the Mongol khans. She was beaten by the Turkish beys. She was beaten by the Swedish feudal lords. She was beaten by the Polish and Lithuanian gentry. She was beaten by the British and French capitalists. She was beaten by the Japanese barons. All beat her — for her backwardness: for military backwardness, for cultural backwardness, for political backwardness, for industrial backwardness, for agricultural backwardness. She was beaten because to do so was profitable and could be done with impunity.

That is why we must no longer lag behind.

In the past we had no motherland, nor could we have one. But now that we have overthrown capitalism and power is in the hands of the working class, we have a motherland and we shall defend its independence. Do you want our socialist motherland to be beaten and to lose its independence? If you do not want this you must end its backwardness in the shortest possible time and develop a genuine Bolshevik tempo in strengthening its socialist economic system. There is no other way. That is why Lenin said during the October Revolution: "Either perish, or catch up with and surpass the advanced capitalist countries." We are fifty or a hundred years behind the advanced countries. We must make good this distance in ten years. Either we do this or they will crush us.

### Results of industrialization

The performance of industry during the 1930s was more gratifying for Stalin than the performance of agriculture:

|  | 1927-28 | 1932 | 1937 |
|---|---|---|---|
| Industrial production (Millions of *rubles*) | 18.3 | 43.3 | 95.5 |
| Electricity (Milliard Kwhs) | 5.05 | 13.4 | 36.2 |
| Coal (Millions of tonnes) | 35.4 | 64.3 | 128.0 |
| Oil ( " " " ) | 11.7 | 21.4 | 28.5 |
| Pig Iron ( " " " ) | 3.3 | 6.2 | 14.5 |
| Steel ( " " " ) | 4.0 | 5.9 | 17.7 |

18 Construction work at Magnitka Hill, 1929. Manual labour was needed to develop industry. This was to become the City of Metallurgists.

19   A government advertisement, in the shape of a
machine, showing the goals of the first Five Year Plan.
The words stress that the fulfilment of the plan will
guarantee the "grandiose expansion of socialist
construction".

To begin with there had been considerable enthusiasm in industry to achieve the goals of the first Five Year Plan (1928-32), but hard work, overcrowding in the factories, bad food and so on had killed this enthusiasm by the mid-1930s. To make people work harder than ever Stalin used a policy of coercion and repression:

> Repressions are a necessary element in the offensive, but an auxiliary, not a principal element,

said Stalin in a speech to a party audience. When machines broke down or production targets were not reached (this happened because the industrial workers lacked skill), Stalin's explanation of the occurrence was simple: there was an enemy, a "wrecker" at work. The "wrecking organizations" who were thus blamed for poor industrial production were described by a Soviet economist, I. Trifonov, in *The Outlines of the History of the Class Struggle in the USSR during NEP:*

> In the course of 1928-31, wrecking organizations were discovered in the following industries: coal mining, defence, textiles, machine, chemical, rubber, oil, in transport and in retail trade. Wreckers appeared in the key institutions of the national economy. They infiltrated the leading bodies of the whole economy: the Supreme Economic Council and the *State Planning Commission.*

## The Great Purge and Show Trials

The assassination of Sergei Kirov, party leader in Leningrad, on 1 December 1934 sparked off what became known later as the Great Purge (1936-38). Millions of people were falsely accused of being enemies of Soviet Russia. They were deported to Siberia and elsewhere and died like flies. From 1936-38 there were many trials of so-called enemies of the Soviet Union, called Show Trials, in which most of the evidence was forged, and which were designed to warn all opponents of the régime against attacking it.

The trial of Bukharin, Tomsky and others took place in March 1938 in Moscow. Bukharin, who had broken down and wept and asked for forgiveness on an earlier date when he had been accused of *factionalism,* stood up strongly to the prosecutor, Vyshinsky, although he knew that the result of the trial would probably be his execution. Vyshinsky asked Bukharin if he had endorsed Trotsky's negotiations to hand over the Ukraine to Germany in 1918:

> *Vyshinsky*: Did you endorse these negotiations?
>
> *Bukharin*: Or disavow? I did not disavow them; consequently I endorsed them.
>
> *Vyshinsky*: I ask you, did you endorse them, or not?
>
> *Bukharin*: I repeat, Citizen Prosecutor: since I did not disavow them, I consequently endorsed them.
>
> *Vyshinsky*: Consequently, you endorsed them?
>
> *Bukharin*: If I did not disavow them, consequently I endorsed them.
>
> *Vyshinsky*: That's what I am asking you: that is to say, you endorsed them?
>
> *Bukharin*: So then "consequently" is the same as "that is to say".
>
> *Vyshinsky*: What do you mean, "that is to say"?
>
> *Bukharin*: That is to say, I endorsed them.
>
> *Vyshinsky*: But you say that you learnt of this *post factum.*
>
> *Bukharin*: Yes, the one does not contradict the other in the slightest.

Vyshinsky questioned Rykov about his knowing some Byelorussians who had been condemned:

> *Vyshinsky*: Isn't this an espionage connection? [knowing the Byelorussians]
>
> *Rykov*: No.

20 Andrei Vyshinsky, the Public Prosecutor. A
former Menshevik, he interpreted Stalin's thoughts
and served him so well that he never fell out of favour.

42

*Vyshinsky*: What kind of connection is it?

*Rykov*: There was an espionage connection there too.

*Vyshinsky*: But was there an espionage connection maintained by a part of your organization with the Poles on your instructions?

*Rykov*: Of course.

*Vyshinsky*: Espionage?

*Rykov*: Of course.

*Vyshinsky*: Bukharin included?

*Rykov*: Of course.

*Vyshinsky*: Were you and Bukharin connected?

*Rykov*: Absolutely.

*Vyshinsky*: So you were spies?

*Rykov*: (no reply)

*Vyshinsky*: And the organizers of the espionage?

△
21   Rykov, Lenin's successor as Chairman of the Sovnarkom (Prime Minister). Part of the "Right" opposition.

*Rykov*: I am in no way better than a spy.

*Vyshinsky*: You organized espionage, so you were spies.

*Rykov*: It may be said, yes.

*Vyshinsky*: It may be said, spies. I am asking, did you organize connections with the Polish intelligence service and the

◁ 22   Bukharin, "the darling of the party", as Lenin called him in his "Testament". The leading economist in the party, he favoured the worker-peasant alliance of NEP and feared that Trotsky and the "Left" opposition would weaken the Soviet Union. He therefore sided with Stalin against them. Then Stalin changed sides.

43

23　Stalin signs a death warrant, 1933.

respective spy circles? Do you plead guilty to espionage?

*Rykov*: If it is a question of organization, then in this case, of course, I plead guilty.

*Vyshinsky*: Accused Bukharin, do you plead guilty to espionage?

*Bukharin*: I do not.

*Vyshinsky*: After what Rykov says, after what Sharangovich [another prisoner] says?

*Bukharin*: I do not plead guilty.

*Vyshinsky*: When the organization of the Rights [counter-revolutionaries] was set up in Byelorussia [a republic of the Soviet Union], you were at the head of it; do you admit that?

*Bukharin*: I have told you.

*Vyshinsky*: I am asking you, do you admit it or not?

*Bukharin*: I took no interest in Byelorussian affairs.

*Vyshinsky*: Did you take an interest in espionage affairs?

*Bukharin*: No.

*Vyshinsky*: And who did take an interest?

*Bukharin*: I received no information with regard to activities of this kind.

*Vyshinsky*: Accused Rykov, was Bukharin receiving any information with regard to activities of this kind?

*Rykov*: I never spoke to him about it.

Rykov had surrendered in his encounter with the Prosecutor, but Bukharin continued to stand up to Vyshinsky.

Many people at the time thought that Stalin was being misled by his advisers, and that he would not have let the show trials go on had he not been receiving false information, from the political police, for example. But this was quite untrue. Here is Stalin's reaction to the news that Kamenev was still refusing to confess (to imaginary crimes), despite all the pressures being brought to bear on him: loss of sleep, semi-starvation, and round-the-clock bullying:

> Now then, don't tell me any longer that Kamenev, or this or that prisoner, is able to withstand such pressure. Don't report back to me until you have Kamenev's confession in your briefcase.

These words are recorded in *Stalin's Crimes* by Alexander Orlov, a former *KGB* officer.

In February 1956, in a speech to the 20th Party Congress, Khrushchev explained the extraordinary events of the 1934-38 period. The speech is known as the "secret speech", because it was made behind closed doors and

24 "Visit the Russian Pyramids" reads this mock travel poster, from a cartoon in an émigré journal. The pyramids are formed of the skulls of all those destroyed by Stalin in the Great Purge.

has never been published in the Soviet Union:

Stalin invented the concept of "enemies of the people". This term made it automatically unnecessary for the ideological errors of a man or men engaged in a controversy to be proved: this then made possible the use of the most cruel oppression, violating all norms of revolutionary legality, against anyone who in any way disagreed with Stalin, against those who were only suspected of hostile intent, against those who had bad reputations. The concept "enemy of the people" actually eliminated the possibility of any kind of ideological struggle or the making of one's views known on this or that issue, even issues of a practical nature.

This led to glaring violations of revolutionary legality and to the fact that many entirely innocent persons, who had in the past defended the party line, became victims. The formula "enemy of the people" was specifically invented to annihilate physically such individuals. Arbitrary behaviour by one person (Stalin) encouraged and permitted arbitrariness by others. Mass arrests, the deportation of many thousands of persons, executions without trial and without normal investigation created a climate of insecurity, fear and even desperation.

# Chapter Four 1941-1945

# Stalin as Warlord

We saw that in 1927 Stalin believed that another war was "on the horizon" and that Britain had "resolutely undertaken to start a war against the Soviet Union". By contrast, in 1941, although Stalin had received warnings of a German attack from the Americans, the British ambassador, Soviet spies in Tokyo, and, on 21 June, from a German army deserter, he refused to believe that the Germans would attack the Soviet Union. He thought there was really no need to fear war.

On 23 August 1939 Stalin had signed the German-Soviet Non-Aggression Pact with Hitler. Under the pact Poland and Europe were divided into German and Soviet zones of influence. Stalin had no intention of breaking the pact, and did not wish to attack Germany; and so, he thought, Hitler must be of the same mind and would not wish to attack the Soviet Union.

## The German attack

Until the very last moment Stalin did not expect a German attack. He expected only "provocations"; in other words, he thought that some German field commanders, acting independently of Hitler, might try to provoke the Soviet Union into attacking Germany:

> The possibility has arisen of a sudden German attack on 21-22 June [1941] . . . .

25 Stalin in c. 1941, aged 63. He is not yet wearing his military uniform. The photographer has found Stalin in a questioning, indeed suspicious mood.

The German attack may begin with provocations . . . . During the night of 21 June occupy secretly the strong points on the frontier . . . disperse and camouflage at special aerodromes . . . have all units battle-ready. No other measures are to be taken without special orders.

This was the message Stalin sent out to the army through Marshal Semyon Timoshenko, Commissar for War, at 12.30 a.m. on Sunday, 22 June 1941. The German army, the Wehrmacht, attacked the Soviet Union along a long front at 4.15 a.m. — before Stalin's message had reached many of the Soviet soldiers.

26 Both Germany and the Soviet Union attacked Poland. This cartoon is a bitter comment on their behaviour. Poland lies prostrate between Hitler and Stalin.

It seems that Stalin retired to his dacha (weekend cottage), suffering from nervous prostration, after the German attack. Eleven days later, however, he was recovered and broadcast this dramatic call to arms:

Comrades, citizens, brothers and sisters, men of our Army and Navy! It is to you I am speaking, dear friends!

The treacherous military attack launched by Hitlerite Germany on our motherland on 22 June, is continuing. In spite of the heroic resistance of the Red Army, and although the enemy's best divisions and best air force units have already been

27 A war poster. Mother-Russia is holding the ▷ military oath, which was sworn by all new conscripts. They swear to defend the Soviet Union with all their strength, indeed to their dying breath. The painter is Irakly Toidze, a Stalin Prize winner.

RENDEZVOUS

48

destroyed and have found their graves on the field of battle, the enemy continues to advance, throwing fresh forces to the front. Hitler's troops have succeeded in capturing Lithuania, most of Latvia, the western part of Byelorussia and part of the Western Ukraine. Fascist aircraft are extending the range of their operations . . . . Grave danger threatens our country.

How has it come about that our glorious Red Army surrendered a number of our cities and districts to the Fascist armies? Is it really true that the Fascist German troops are unbeatable, as the boastful Fascist propagandists are endlessly claiming? Of course not! History proves that there are no unbeatable armies and there never have been unbeatable armies.

It may be asked, how could the Soviet government have agreed to sign a Non-Aggression Pact with such treacherous people, such monsters, as Hitler and Ribbentrop? Was this not a mistake by the Soviet government? Of course not! I think that no peace-loving state would decline a peace agreement with a neighbouring state, even though the latter was headed by such monsters and cannibals as Hitler and Ribbentrop.

The Red Army, the Red Navy and all Soviet citizens must defend every inch of Soviet soil, must fight to the last drop of blood for our towns and villages, must demonstrate the daring, initiative and mental awareness for which our people

28 A scene from the Russian documentary film *The Great Patriotic War*. On the airfield a brilliant young pianist gives a concert to the aircrew before they go into battle.

are known. We must wage a ruthless struggle against all disorganizers of the rear, deserters, panic-mongers and rumour-mongers; we must destroy all spies, saboteurs and enemy parachutists, affording rapid help to our extermination batallions. If Red Army units are forced to retreat, all rolling stock must be evacuated; the enemy must not be left a single engine, a single railway wagon, a single pound of grain or litre of fuel. Collective farmers must drive away their cattle . . . . All valuable property, including non-ferrous metals, grain and fuel, which cannot be moved, must be destroyed without fail.

All our strength for the support of our heroic Red Army and our glorious Red Navy!

All the forces of the people for the destruction of the enemy! Forward to victory!

From this time onwards Stalin threw himself into the war, as war leader. He never left Moscow, except between 16 and 18 October 1941. Even when most of the party and government, fearing that the Germans might capture Moscow, left for Kuibyshev in the Urals, Stalin remained in Moscow.

### The early months of the war

Why did the Red Army do so badly in the early months of the war? It lacked leaders, and for this Stalin was largely responsible. For during the Great Purge he had had shot:

29   The caption to this German cartoon of 1941 reads: "Am I dreaming or is this real?" It shows the Russian "steamroller" (the Red Army) driven by Stalin smashed in a collision with the German swastika (the Wehrmacht).

30 A battery outside the Theatre of the Soviet Army, Moscow, 1941.

three of the five Marshals of the Soviet Union; three of the four full generals; all twelve lieutenant generals; sixty of the sixty-seven corps commanders; and one hundred and thirty-six of the one hundred and ninety-nine divisional commanders. The top ranks of the Navy had been even more savagely decimated. Ironically the crime they had been accused of during the Great Purge was being German and Japanese spies. No evidence has yet come to light to prove this accusation.

There was also a shortage of weapons. On the first day of the war, Khrushchev, who was then head of the party in the Ukraine, telephoned from the capital, Kiev, to Moscow, asking for weapons. In his *Memoirs* he recalled the telephone conversation he had had with Malenkov, the chief in charge of armaments production during the war and Stalin's number two:

*Khrushchev*: Tell me, when can we get rifles? There are factory workers here who wish to join the ranks of the Red Army to fight the Germans and we haven't got any arms for them.

*Malenkov*: You'd better abandon any thought of getting rifles from us. The rifles in the civil defence organization here have all been sent to Leningrad.

*Khrushchev*: Then what are we supposed to fight with?

*Malenkov*: I don't know. Pikes, swords, homemade weapons, anything you can make in your own factories.

*Khrushchev*: You mean we should fight tanks with spears?

*Malenkov*: You'll have to do the best you can. You can make incendiary bombs out of bottles of petrol or kerosene and throw them at the tanks.

## Stalin as war leader

On 19 July 1941 Stalin nominated himself and was appointed Commissar for War. Timoshenko became a field commander. On 7 August Stalin named himself Commander-in-Chief. Now he was supreme war leader, but he was not always good at choosing his top men. Voroshilov was made commander-in-chief of the Northern Front, Budyonny of the Southern Front and Timoshenko of the Central Front. Budyonny was not an ideally efficient and organized war leader, as is obvious here from his explanation of how he had got lost and had lost his troops. This happened in late summer 1941. Zhukov had been sent to find Budyonny:

*Budyonny*: Where have you come from?

*Zhukov*: From Konev's headquarters.

*Budyonny*: Well, how are things with him? I lost contact with him two days ago. Yesterday I was at the Forty-Third Army HQ. In my absence the staff of my front moved, and now I don't know where they are.

This conversation was recorded by Khrushchev in his *Memoirs*.

On the eve of the twenty-fourth anniversary of the revolution, 6 November 1941, Stalin spoke to a Moscow soviet and party audience and painted a realistic picture of the situation.

I have already said in one of my public speeches at the beginning of the war that the war was a dangerous threat to our country . . . . Now after four months of war, I must emphasize that this danger has not diminished but has even increased. The enemy stops at no sacrifice, he does not care one jot for the blood of his soldiers . . . . In four months of war we have lost 350 000 killed, and 378 000 missing, and our wounded number 1 020 000. In the same period the enemy has lost more than 4 500 000 men killed,

wounded and taken prisoner.

Stalin's figures were not exact. The strains of war probably made him distort them. Actually, the Red Army lost 3 200 000 men and the Germans 750 000 men over the period.

Khrushchev was called to Moscow at the end of 1941 and, as he wrote in his *Memoirs*, found that Stalin was

much changed . . . . He revealed all the strong-willed determination of the heroic leader. But I knew what sort of leader he was. I'd seen him when he had been paralyzed by his fear of Hitler, like a rabbit in front of a boa constrictor. During the first part of the war, when things were going badly for us, I did not fail to notice that Stalin's signature never appeared on a single document or order. This practice didn't change even when we drove the Germans back from Moscow [December 1941] and Stalin began to regain his self-confidence. And this was no accident. Nothing Stalin ever did was an accident.

Normally, Stalin's name would have appeared under everything he wrote or said. However, his orders at the beginning of the war never bore his name, so that he could not be blamed afterwards if the order led to failure.

The Germans were defeated at Moscow in March 1942, but were still besieging Leningrad when a major battle developed at Kharkov in May 1942. Khrushchev was closely involved in the planning of this battle and realized very early on that it would be a disastrous one for the Soviet Union. He therefore ordered an end to the offensive. Stalin overruled him, saying that the battle should go on. Khrushchev tried desperately to contact Stalin in order to convince him that the offensive was a mistake. He told in his *Memoirs* of how he had had a further telephone conversation with Malenkov (page 52):

I called the dacha and Malenkov answered. We exchanged greetings, and then I asked:

31 A Polish woman polishes glasses in an officers' messroom. The room is dominated by the Stalin portrait, in which his pock marks have been painted out.

"May I speak to comrade Stalin?" Stalin must have been there . . . . I could hear Malenkov saying that I was on the telephone and asking to speak to Stalin. Malenkov said: "Comrade Stalin says you should tell me what you want and I'll pass on the message." This was a sure sign of trouble. So I had to tell Malenkov that by continuing the offensive we would be playing right into the enemy's hands.

"There's no point in discussing it further. Stalin says that the offensive must continue."

Malenkov hung up. Comrade Bagramyan

was with me and overheard the conversation. His nerves cracked and he burst into tears. He could see what was going to happen. He was weeping for our army.

## The Allies of the Soviet Union

Great Britain became an ally following the German attack on the Soviet Union in June 1941. The United States of America became an ally against Germany after the Japanese attack on Pearl Harbour in December 1941 and the German declaration of war.

Winston Churchill, the British Prime Minister, described his meeting with Stalin to the House of Commons:

It was an experience of great interest to me to meet Premier Stalin. . . . It is very fortunate for Russia in her agony to have this great rugged chief at her head. He is a

32 Semyon Mikhailovich Budyonny — first-class as a cavalry officer in the Civil War, but hopeless when confronted by German tanks.

33 Georgy Konstantinovich Zhukov, one of the heroes of the war. A great commander but a very rude man. Stalin became jealous of his popularity and moved him away from the limelight in 1946.

man of outstanding personality, suited to the sombre and stormy times in which his life has been cast. He is a man of inexhaustible courage and will-power, a man direct and even blunt in speech . . . above all, with that saving sense of humour which is of high importance to all men and to all nations. Premier Stalin also left upon me an impression of deep cool wisdom and a complete absence of illusions of any kind.

In the next chapter you will find what Stalin says about Churchill.

Harry Hopkins, President Roosevelt's confidential adviser, described Stalin just after he had met him, as:

an austere, rugged, determined figure in boots that shone like mirrors, stout baggy trousers and snug-fitting blouse. He wore no ornament . . . . He's built close to the ground, like a football coach's dream of a tackle.

## The end of the War

The fortunes of war changed dramatically for the good for the Soviet Union in 1943. The tremendous Soviet victory at Stalingrad in February, the crushing of the Germans at Kursk in the summer (the greatest tank battle ever) and the failure of the Wehrmacht to take Leningrad all signalled the beginning of the end for Hitler's armies.

Stalin had something to boast about, when he spoke to a Moscow soviet and party audience on 6 November 1943:

34 A meeting of the Allies at Tehran, Persia, in December 1943. Sarah Churchill, the Prime Minister's daughter, is being presented to Stalin. Behind her (partly hidden) is Molotov. Behind Roosevelt is Averell Harriman, and behind Churchill is Anthony Eden (later Lord Avon).

35 A German cartoon of July 1941, in which Roosevelt and Churchill gasp "We can't support him!" The implication was that the USA and Great Britain could not prevent the defeat of the Soviet Union.

36　At the Yalta Conference of the Big Three (UK, USA and USSR), February, 1945. Stalin in conversation with President F.D. Roosevelt.

The past year, between the twenty-fifth and the twenty-sixth anniversaries of the October Revolution, marked a turn in the *Great Fatherland War* . . . . As a result of these offensives in the course of the last year our troops were able to fight their way forward from 500 kilometres in the central part of the front up to 1 300 kilometres in the south and to liberate almost one million square kilometres of territory — that is, almost two-thirds of the Soviet land temporarily seized by the enemy.

At last, victory came. Stalin broadcast the following message on 9 May 1945. (Because Moscow time was one hour ahead of Berlin time, the date of Victory in Europe Day is a day later than in the rest of Europe itself.)

Comrades! Compatriots!
　The great day of victory over Germany, over Fascist Germany, forced to her knees by the Red Army and the armies of our allies, has arrived. She has acknowledged defeat and has surrendered unconditionally.
　The great sacrifices made by us in the name of freedom and the independence of our motherland, the innumerable hardships and sufferings, experienced by our

people in the course of the war, the intensive work at the front and in the rear, placed on the altar of our fatherland, has not been in vain and has been crowned with complete victory over the enemy. The centuries-long struggle of the Slav peoples for their existence and their independence has ended with victory over the German invaders and German tyranny.

Comrades, the Great Fatherland War has ended with complete victory to us. The period of war in Europe is over. The period of peaceful development has dawned.

I congratulate you, my dear compatriots, on our victory.

Glory to our heroic Red Army which has defended the independence of our motherland and achieved victory over the enemy!

Glory to our great people, our victorious people!

Eternal glory to the heroes who fell in the battles with the enemy and gave their lives for the freedom and happiness of our people!

Stalin later stated that the war had cost the Soviet Union twenty million dead — soldiers, prisoners-of-war and civilians. The numbers in the Red Army more than doubled between the beginning and the end of the war:

| | |
|---|---|
| 22 June 1941 | 2 900 000 men |
| 1 December 1941 | 4 200 000 men |
| 1 May 1942 | 5 500 000 men |
| 1 November 1942 | 6 124 000 men |
| 1 July 1943 | 6 442 000 men |
| 1 January 1944 | 6 100 000 men |
| 1 January 1945 | 6 000 000 men |

The civilian population had also played a major part in the victory by producing armaments. This table shows a comparison of the Soviet and the German war effort:

| ARMAMENTS PRODUCED | SOVIET UNION 1 July 1941—30 June 1945 | GERMANY 1941-44 |
|---|---|---|
| Rifles and carbines | 12,000,000 | 7,500,000 |
| Submachine guns | 6,103,000 | 1,247,000 |
| Light and heavy machine guns | 954,500 | 617,000 |
| Mortars | 347,900 | 68,000 |
| Field guns (75 mm and over) | 97,768 | 44,800 |
| Tanks and self-propelled guns | 95,099 | 53,800 |
| Combat aircraft | 108,028 | 78,900 |

# Russian defence lines in the Great Fatherland War

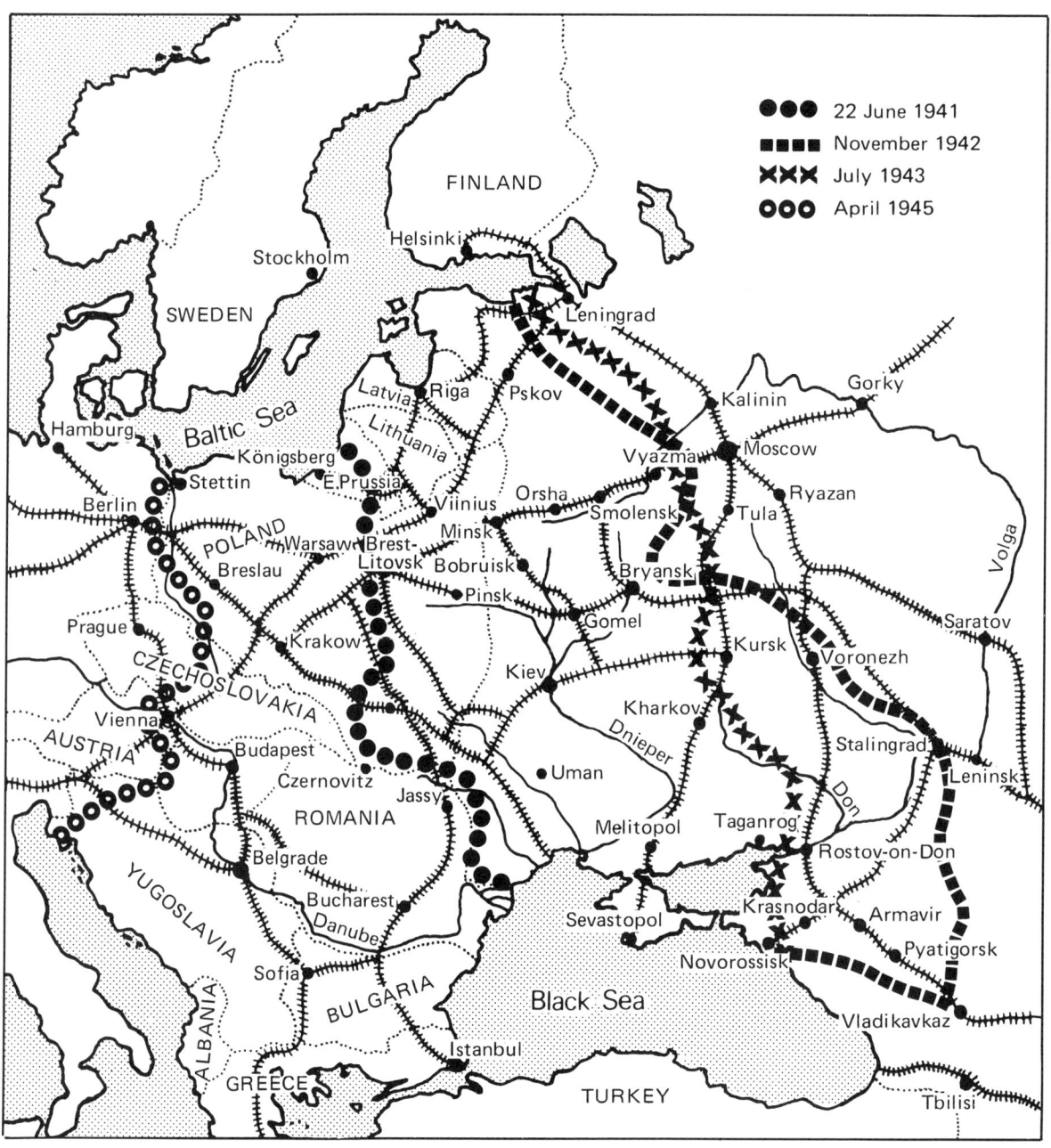

Legend:
- ●●● 22 June 1941
- ■■■ November 1942
- XXX July 1943
- ○○○ April 1945

# Chapter Five 1945-1953

# Stalin's Last Years

## Industrialization and Collectivization

People had hoped that once the war was won, there might be a change in policy about industrialization and collectivization. However, these hopes were dashed when Stalin, in a speech delivered on 9 February 1946 to an election meeting in Moscow, made clear that rapid industrialization and collectivization had come to stay and that great sacrifices were to be asked of the Soviet population even in peacetime. Note how he addresses the audience and compare the speech with that of 3 July 1941 (page 48):

Comrades!
. . . What then, are the results of the war?

First and foremost, our victory means that our Soviet *social* structure has triumphed, our Soviet *social* structure has successfully stood up to the test, in the fires of war and has completely shown its viability. . . .

Secondly, our victory means that our Soviet *state* structure, that our multinational Soviet state has come through all the trials of war and has shown its viability . .

Thirdly, our victory shows that our Soviet armed forces, our Red Army, has triumphed, that the Red Army has heroically survived all the setbacks of the war, has smashed our enemies' armies and has emerged as the victor from the war.

(Cry from the hall: "Under the leadership of comrade Stalin!" All stand, stormy, uninterrupted applause, becoming an ovation.)

What material potential did our country enjoy before the Second World War? [Stalin then gives a very long list of agricultural and industrial production figures.]

What policy permitted the Communist Party to provide this material potential in such a short time?

First of all, the Soviet policy of the industrialization of the country . . . .

Secondly, the policy of the collectivization of agriculture . . . .

Now for a few words about the work plans of the Communist Party in the near future. As you know, these plans are laid down in the new Five Year Plan which is soon to be confirmed . . . . As far as plans for the longer term are concerned, the party intends to organize a new expansion of the economy which will make it possible for us, for example, to treble output compared with the pre-war period. We have to do this so that our industry can produce annually about 50 million tonnes of pig iron, about 60 million tonnes of steel, about 500 million tonnes of coal and about 60 million tonnes of oil. Only under these conditions can we consider that our

motherland will be protected against all accidents. This will take, let us say, three more Five Year Plans, if not more. But this can be done and we must do it.

62

△
37 Stalin as he wished others to see him. An idealized picture of the Soviet leader at the end of the war. He was very aware of his shortness, hence did not like this emphasized.

## The "Iron Curtain"

After 1945 Soviet influence in Eastern Europe expanded. Eastern Europe was being communized. Many Western European statesmen became anxious about this. Winston Churchill, out of office, made a speech at Fulton, Missouri, USA, on 6 March 1946, in which he talked of an "iron curtain", which was descending on Europe from the Baltic to the Adriatic. Events behind the "iron curtain" could not be influenced by the West. Stalin's response to this idea was

38 A *Daily Mail* cartoon on Churchill's "iron curtain" speech. Joe is Stalin.

PEEP UNDER THE IRON CURTAIN

△
39　Western statesmen feared that the same fate would overtake Eastern Europe as had befallen Estonia, Latvia and Lithuania. These republics, shown here as the children who followed the Pied Piper (Stalin), had been forcibly annexed to the Soviet Union in 1940

published in an interview with a *Pravda* correspondent on 14 March 1946:

　*Question*: What do you think of Mr Churchill's latest speech, delivered in the United States?

　*Answer*: I regard it as a dangerous move, calculated to sow discord among the

Allied states and to make co-operation difficult.

*Question*: Can it be said that Mr Churchill's speech endangers peace and security?

*Answer*: Without question. Basically, Mr Churchill has taken up the position of a war-monger. And Mr Churchill is not alone in this. He has friends not only in England but also in the United States.

It should be mentioned that Mr Churchill and his friends are strikingly reminiscent in this respect of Hitler and his friends. Hitler began the unleashing of war by proclaiming a racial theory which stated that only those who spoke German formed a true nation. Mr Churchill is also beginning the unleashing of a war with a racial theory, that only nations which speak English are truly nations, elected to decide the fate of the world. The German theory of race led Hitler and his friends to the conclusion that nations which speak German are the only true nations and hence must rule the other nations of the world.

*Question*: What do you think of that part of Mr Churchill's speech in which he attacks the democratic structure of those European states which are our neighbours and in which he criticizes the good-neighbourly mutual assistance which exists between these states and the Soviet Union?

*Answer*: This part of Mr Churchill's speech is a mixture of slander, crudity and lack of tact.

## Interest in Linguistics

Linguistics is not a subject which is usually regarded as having any political significance. Politicians would not be expected to be concerned about the study of language. However, Stalin did take an involved interest in language towards the end of his life, and he gave the subject a political meaning.

Stalin said that the political, legal, religious, artistic and philosophical views of a society all depended on the economic structure at the time. He called the economic structure of a society its "base", and all the ideas which depended on it he called its "super-structure". Language was more important than both the base and the superstructure because it was more long-lasting:

The superstructure is the product of one epoch, during which a particular economic base exists and functions. For this reason the life of a superstructure is not long; it is liquidated and disappears with the liquidation and disappearance of the particular base.

Language, on the contrary, is the product of a whole series of epochs, over the period of which it is formed, enriched, developed, polished. For this reason language lives much longer than any base or superstructure .... Language is directly linked to the productive activity of man, and not only to productive activity, but to every other activity of man in all spheres of his work, from production to base, from base to superstructure. Due to this, language reflects changes in production immediately and directly, without waiting for changes in the base ....

Therefore: (a) a Marxist cannot consider language part of the superstructure

(b) to confuse language with the super-structure is to commit a serious error.

This extract, showing that Stalin involved himself in issues which were not normally regarded as political, is taken from five letters which he published in the summer of 1950.

## Relations with China

Since the Soviet Union had helped China defeat Japan on 2 September 1945, Stalin had written a letter of congratulation to China on each anniversary of the defeat. On the sixth anniversary of the defeat of

Japan Stalin's letter to the Chinese leader, Mao Tse-tung, was also published in *Pravda*:

I thank you, comrade chairman, for your high valuation of the role of the Soviet Union and its armed forces in the destruction of the aggressive Japanese forces.
[ Stalin had received a telegram from Mao Tse-tung, thanking the Soviet Union for its help in the Japanese defeat.]

The Chinese people and its Liberation Army, irrespective of the machinations of the Kuomintang, played an important role in liquidating the Japanese imperialists. The struggle of the Chinese people and its Liberation Army made the destruction of the aggressive Japanese forces much easier.

There is no doubt that the indestructible friendship of the Soviet Union and the Chinese People's Republic serves and will serve to guarantee peace in the Far East against all and every aggressor and war-monger.

I ask you, comrade chairman, to accept the greetings of the Soviet Union and its armed forces on the occasion of the sixth anniversary of the liberation of Eastern Asia from the yoke of Japanese imperialism.

Long live the great friendship between the Chinese People's Republic and the Soviet Union!

Long live the Chinese People's Liberation Army!

Chairman of the USSR Council of
Ministers
J. Stalin
2 September 1951

How things have changed since Stalin spoke of the "indestructible friendship" between China and the Soviet Union!

## Stalin's last speech

Stalin's last known public speech was delivered to the nineteenth Congress of the Communist Party of the Soviet Union on 14 October 1952:

Comrades!
Permit me, in the name of our congress, to express our thanks to all the fraternal parties and groups whose representatives have honoured our congress with their presence. It would be a mistake to think that our party, which is now a mighty power, no longer needs support. This is not true. Our party and our country always has and always will need the trust, sympathy and support of fraternal peoples abroad . . .

Special attention must be paid to those communist, democratic or worker-peasant parties which have not yet come to power and still labour under the heel of Draconic bourgeois laws. Of course, it is more difficult for them to work. However, it is not as difficult for them to work as it was for us, Russian communists under Tsarist rule.

Why is it not as difficult for these parties to work compared with the Russian communists of the Tsarist régime?

Firstly, because they have before their eyes the examples of struggle and success in the Soviet Union and the people's democracies. Consequently they can learn from the mistakes and successes of these countries and thereby make their own task easier.

## Death of Stalin

The following items tell of the death of Stalin:

*Medical Report of the Illness and Death of J. V. Stalin*

On the night of 2 March 1953, J.V. Stalin suffered a haemorrhage of the brain (left hemisphere) due to hypertonia and arteriosclerosis. As a result, paralysis of the left side and loss of consciousness occurred . . . . On the afternoon of 5 March the condition of the patient deteriorated very quickly, breathing became shallow and much faster, the pulse reached 140-150 beats per minute and the blood pressure dropped.

At 21.50 hours with cardiac failure growing and breathing becoming less and less frequent, J.V. Stalin died.

(*Pravda*, 6 March 1953)

This medical report of Stalin's death was printed in *Pravda* alongside the notice of Stalin's death from the Central Committee of the Communist Party of the Soviet Union, the USSR Council of Ministers and the USSR *Supreme Soviet*. This read:

Dear Comrades and Friends,
The Central Committee of the Communist Party of the Soviet Union, the USSR Council of Ministers and the USSR Supreme Soviet announce with deep sorrow to the party and all working people of the Soviet Union that at 9.50 p.m. on 5 March, Joseph Vissarionovich STALIN, Chairman of the USSR Council of Ministers and Secretary of the Central Committee of the Communist Party of the Soviet Union, died after a serious illness.

The heart of Lenin's comrade-in-arms, the inspired continuer of Lenin's work, the wise leader and teacher of the Communist Party of the Soviet Union — Joseph Vissarionovich STALIN — has stopped beating.

The news of comrade STALIN's death will bring great pain to the hearts of the workers, collective farmers, intelligentsia and all the working people of our motherland, to the hearts of the warriors of our glorious army and navy, to the hearts of millions of working people in all countries of the world.

And let us leave the last word to Stalin's daughter, Svetlana Alliluyeva. Her description of Stalin's death appeared in *Twenty Letters to a Friend by Svetlana Alliluyeva,* published in 1967:

When we were through the gates, Khrushchev and Bulganin waved my car to stop in the drive outside the dacha.

40   Svetlana Alliluyeva, Stalin's daughter

I thought it must be all over. They took me by the arm as I got out. They were both in tears.

Even in the front hall nothing was the same as usual. Instead of the normal deep silence, everyone was fussing and running around. When someone finally told me that my father had had a stroke during the night and was unconscious, I even felt a little relieved. I had thought that he was already dead. Apparently, it had happened during the night. They found him at three in the morning, in this room, right here, lying on a rug by the sofa. They decided to carry him to the next room, to the sofa he usually slept on. That is where he was now. The doctors were in there, too, "You may go in," someone said to me.

I listened in a daze. The details no longer had any meaning. I could take in only one thing: he was dying. I hadn't yet spoken to the doctors but I didn't

67

doubt it for a second. I could just see that this whole house and everything around me was dying already before my eyes. All the three days I was there I saw only this one thing. It was obvious that there couldn't be any other outcome.

It's a strange thing but during these days of illness when he was nothing but a body out of which the soul had flown . . . I loved my father more tenderly than I had ever before. He'd been very remote from me, from us, his children and all his relatives. During the past few years enormous blown-up photographs of children, a little boy on skis, a boy in a blossoming cherry tree, had appeared in his rooms at the dacha, but he hadn't once found the time to see five of his eight grandchildren. Yet even the grandchildren who never saw him loved him and love him still. During those days when he found peace at last on his deathbed and his face became beautiful and serene, I felt my heart breaking from grief and love.

**Key to Map of the Soviet Union**

| | | | |
|---|---|---|---|
| 1 | RSFSR | 9 | Moldavia |
| 2 | Ukraine | 10 | Latvia |
| 3 | Byelorussia | 11 | Kirghizia |
| 4 | Uzbekistan | 12 | Tadzhikistan |
| 5 | Kazakhstan | 13 | Armenia |
| 6 | Georgia | 14 | Turkmenistan |
| 7 | Azerbaidzhan | 15 | Estonia |
| 8 | Lithuania | | | |

# Map of the Soviet Union

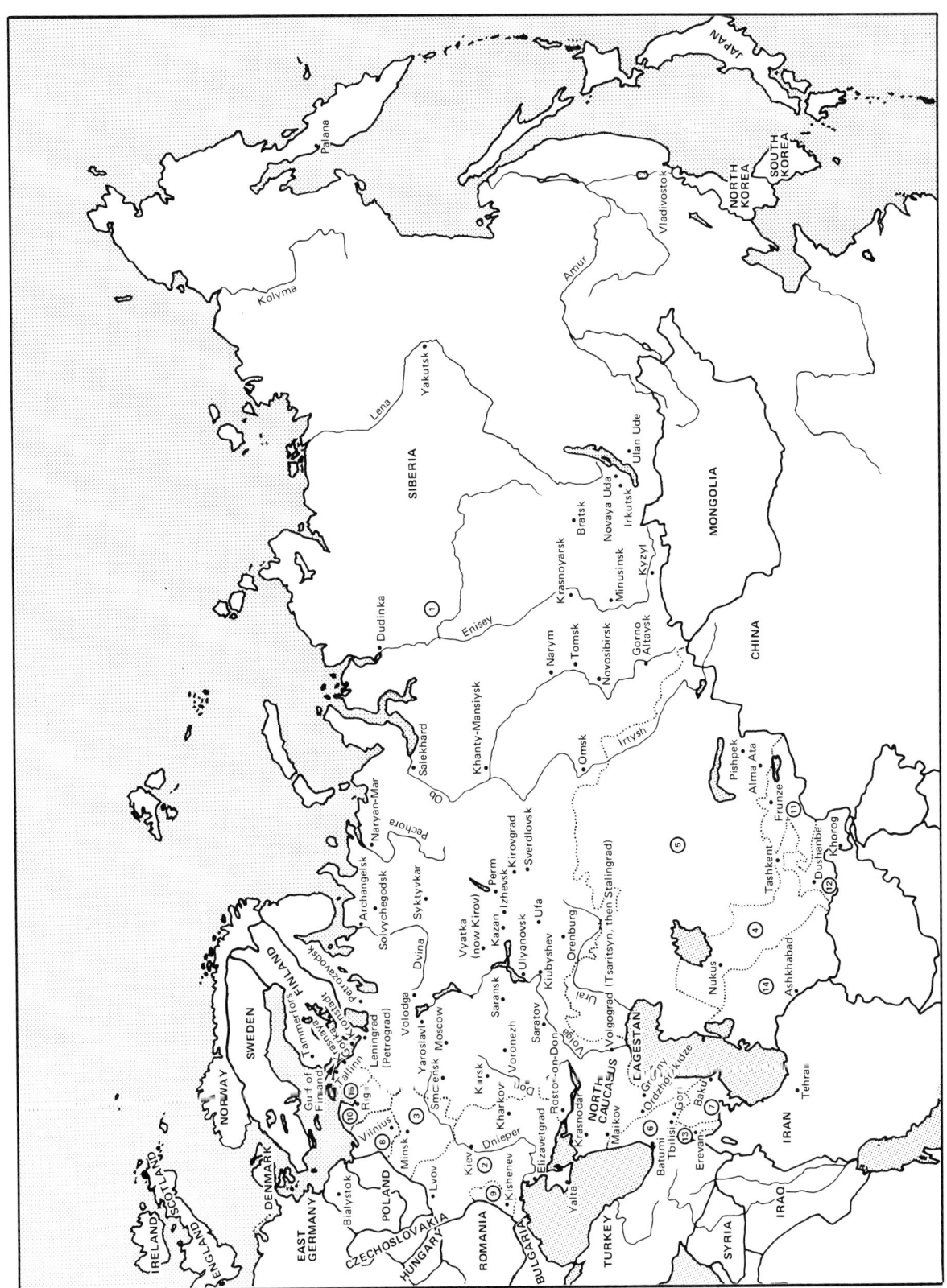

# List of Dates of Stalin's Activities

**Childhood and Education**

| | | |
|---|---|---|
| 1879 | 21 December | Joseph Vissarionovich Djugashvili (Stalin) born in Gori, Georgia, the Caucasus; fourth child of Vissarion Ivanovich Djugashvili, shoemaker, and Ekaterina Georgievna Djugashvili (née Geladze) |
| 1890 | | Enters Gori Theological School. Father dies. |
| 1894 | | Enters Tbilisi Theological Seminary. |
| 1898 | | Joins Tbilisi Marxist group. |
| 1899 | 10 June | Expelled from Tbilisi Theological Seminary shortly before graduation for not attending examinations. |
| 1900 | | Gets job in Tbilisi Observatory. |

**Early Political Activities** Page 7

| | | |
|---|---|---|
| 1900 | 1 May | Makes first public speech about the political situation, for the Marxists, in Tbilisi |
| 1901 | 22 March | Loses job at Tbilisi Observatory and is sought by the police for illegal political activities. Goes "underground" in Tbilisi. |
| | 24 November | Elected member of Tbilisi Social Democratic Committee. |
| 1902 | 17 April | Arrested for illegal political activities. |
| 1903 | 25 July | Sentenced to three years' exile in Siberia. |
| | November | Starts journey to Siberia. |
| 1904 | January | Arrives in Novaya Uda, Irkutsk Province to begin exile. |
| | February | Escapes, returns to Tbilisi and marries Ekaterina Svanidze. |
| 1905 | May | First pamphlet, *Briefly About Party Differences* is published. |
| | 24-30 December | Attends 1st All-Russian Bolshevik Conference at Tammerfors, Finland, as delegate from the Caucasus, and meets Lenin for the first time. |
| 1906 | 15 April | Arrested but released. |
| | 23 April-8 May | Attends 4th Congress of the RSDLP in Stockholm, Sweden. |
| 1907 | 13 May-1 June | Attends 5th Congress of the RSDLP in London. |
| 1908 | 16 March | Yakov, a son, born. |
| | 7 April | Arrested and imprisoned in Baku. |
| | November | Exiled to Solvychegodsk, Vologda Province. |

| | | |
|---|---|---|
| 1909 | July | Escapes from Solvychegodsk and returns to Baku under pseudonym Zakhar Gregorian Melikyants. |
| | | Wife dies of pneumonia. |
| 1910 | 5 April | Arrested in Baku. |
| | 6 October | Exiled to Solvychegodsk, Vologda Province. |
| 1911 | June | Elected in absentio member of the Organization Committee in Russia of the All-Russian Conference of the RSDLP. |
| | | Completes exile in Solvychegodsk. Agrees with police to reside in Vologda but moves to St Petersburg under pseudonym Chizhikov. |
| | 22 September | Arrested in St Petersburg. |
| | December | Exiled to Vologda, Vologda Province. |
| 1912 | February | Co-opted as member of the CC of the RSDLP — proposed by Lenin. |
| | 13 March | Escapes from Vologda. |
| | 5 May | First issue of *Pravda*, the new legal party newspaper, appears. Had worked on it. |
| | | Arrested in St Petersburg for illegal political activities. |
| | 14 July | Exiled to Narym Territory, Tomsk Province. |
| | 14 September | Escapes to St Petersburg under pseudonym Vasilyev. |
| 1913 | January-February | In Krakow, Poland and Vienna, Austria, to write pamphlet on the nationalities problem, under the guidance of Lenin and helped by Bukharin. |
| | 8 March | Arrested in St Petersburg. |
| | July | Exiled to Turukhan Territory, Arctic Circle. |
| 1916 | December | Called to Krasnoyarsk to report for army medical. |
| 1917 | February | Rejected for service as medically unfit (possibly on account of stiff elbow). |

**The "February Revolution"** Page 7

| | | |
|---|---|---|
| 1917 | 25 March | Arrives in Petrograd (formerly St Petersburg) and works on *Pravda*. |
| | 10 April | Makes major speech at All-Russian Conference of Bolsheviks, on the official Bolshevik policy towards the Provisional Government. |
| | 7-12 May | Elected member of CC at 7th All-Russian Conference of the RSDLP. |
| | 24 July | Becomes go-between between the CC in Petrograd and Lenin, who is in hiding in Finland. |
| | 8-16 August | Attends 6th Congress of the RSDLP, Petrograd and is elected to the CC. |

**The "October Revolution", 7 November, and founding of the first Bolshevik Government, the Sovnarkom, 8 November 1917** Page 11

| | | |
|---|---|---|
| 1917 | 8 November | Becomes Chairman for Nationalities in the Sovnarkom. |
| | 12 December | Elected by the CC as one of the Bureau of Four to deal with immediate party problems. Other three are Lenin, Trotsky and Sverdlov. |

| 1918 | 6-8 March | Elected to the CC at 7th Congress of the RSDLP. Party renamed Russian Communist Party (Bolsheviks). |
| | 29 May | Put in charge of providing food for northern Russia, including Moscow and Petrograd. |

## The Civil War, June 1918-December 1920 Page 12

| 1918 | 4 June | Leaves Moscow for Tsaritsyn with armed guard (as Tsaritsyn was a White area) to collect grain. |
| | 6 June | Arrives in Tsaritsyn with 450-man guard. |
| | 16 June | Sends first shipment of food to Moscow by water. |
| | 19 July | Made member of War Council of Southern Front. |
| | 12 September | Leaves Tsaritsyn to go to Moscow. |
| | 22 September | Returns to Tsaritsyn. |
| | 5 October | Recalled from Tsaritsyn by Lenin on Trotsky's request, removed from War Council of Southern Front. Goes to Moscow to see Lenin and Sverdlov, the President of Soviet Russia. |
| | 11 October | Returns to Tsaritsyn. |
| | 19 October | Leaves Tsaritsyn for good. |
| | 6 November | Publishes anniversary article in *Pravda* stating that Trotsky was directly in charge of the October uprising and was mainly responsible for its success. (He was trying to prove that his disagreement with Trotsky was over.) |
| | 30 November | Becomes member of Supreme War Council. |
| 1919 | 5 January | Arrives in Vyatka with Dzerzhinsky and begins purge of the Red Army, to solve problems of poor leadership, delinquency, etc. |
| | 4 February | Declines to become member of War Council of South West Front. Remains in Moscow, where his position would be stronger. |
| | 2-6 March | Delegate to the 1st Congress of the Comintern. (Other Russian delegates are Lenin, Trotsky, Zinoviev, Bukharin.) |
| | 18-23 March | Attends 8th Congress of RCP(B), and is elected to the Politburo, set up for the first time. |
| | 15 May | Sent to Petrograd to help Zinoviev defend the city against the White General Yudenich. |
| | 27 November | Awarded the Order of the Red Banner for his services in defence of Petrograd and on the Southern Front. |
| 1920 | 3 February | Declines to become member of War Council of the Caucasian Front. Remains in Moscow. |
| | 13 November | Proclaims autonomy of Daghestan, in capacity of Chairman for Nationalities. |

## After the Civil War Page 16

| 1921 | 15 February | Red Army invades Georgia and brings down Menshevik government. Stalin, acting in his capacity of Chairman for Nationalities, is the prime mover in this aggression. (Trotsky, Commissar for War, is in the Urals and is not consulted. Stalin receives his authority from Lenin.) |
| | 8-16 March | Attends 10th Congress of RCP(B). Is re-elected member of |

|      |                    | Politburo and of Orgburo. |
|------|--------------------|---------------------------|
| 1922 | 27 March-2 April   | Attends 11th Congress of the RCP(B). Is re-elected to Politburo and elected Secretary General of the CC. |

## Decline of Lenin (first stroke 26 May 1922)

| 1922 | 16 December | Following Lenin's second stroke, becomes one of the triumvirate (group of three) to take his place. Others are Zinoviev and Kamenev. |
|------|-------------|------|
| 1923 | February    | Tells Trotsky, Zinoviev and Kamenev that Lenin has asked him for poison (probably to give them the impression that Lenin's balance of mind was disturbed). |
|      | 5-6 March   | Receives letter dictated by Lenin, threatening to break off all relations with him. |
|      | 17-25 April | Attends 12th Congress of the RCP(B). Becomes senior successor to Lenin, who has had his third stroke on 9 March. |

## Death of Lenin, 21 January 1924 Page 19

| 1924 | 26 January | Makes speech to 2nd All-Union Congress of Soviets in which he swears to uphold Lenin's views. |
|------|------------|------|
|      | 23 May     | Attends 13th Party Congress of the RCP(B). Re-elected to Politburo and Orgburo; also elected Secretary General. |

## Elimination of Stalin's rivals Pages 24-8

| 1925 | 17 January       | Has Trotsky removed as Commissar for War. |
|------|------------------|------|
|      | 18-31 December   | Attends 14th Congress of the RCP(B), at which Zinoviev is defeated. |
| 1926 | 12 February      | Zinoviev replaced as party leader in Leningrad by Sergei Kirov, supporter of Stalin. |
|      | 23 July          | Zinoviev expelled from Politburo. |
|      | 23 October       | Trotsky and Kamenev expelled from Politburo. |
| 1927 | 12 November      | Trotsky and Zinoviev expelled from communist party, Kamenev and others expelled from CC. |
|      | 2-19 December    | Attends 15th Congress of AUCP(B). Re-elected to Politburo and Orgburo, and as Secretary General. |
| 1928 | 16 January       | Trotsky exiled to Alma Ata on Chinese frontier. |
| 1929 | 18 January       | Decision taken to expel Trotsky from the USSR. |
|      | 3 July           | Bukharin dismissed as head of the Comintern. |
|      | 17 November      | Bukharin expelled from the Politburo. |
| 1930 | 26 June-13 July  | Attends 16th Congress of AUCP(B). Re-elected to Politburo and Orgburo, and as Secretary General. |
|      | 20 December      | Rykov succeeded by Molotov as Chairman of the Council of People's Commissars (Sovnarkom) (Prime Minister). |
|      | 21 December      | Rykov expelled from Politburo, succeeded by Ordzhonikidze. |
| 1932 | 8 November       | Second wife, Nadezhda, commits suicide. |
| 1934 | 26 January-10 February | Attends 17th Congress of the AUCP(B) and is hailed as a genius. |

## The Great Purge and Show Trials Page 41

| 1934 | 1 December | Kirov assassinated. |
|------|------------|---------------------|
| 1935 | 15-16 January | Show trial of nineteen (Zinoviev, Kamenev and others). |
| 1936 | 11-24 August | Show trial of sixteen (Zinoviev, Kamenev and others). All defendants executed. |
| 1937 | 23-30 January | Show trial of seventeen; thirteen executed. |
|      | 12 June | Tukhachevsky and seven other famous Red Army generals executed. |
| 1938 | 2-13 March | Show trial of twenty-one; eighteen executed. |
| 1939 | 4 May | Molotov succeeds Litvinov as Foreign Minister. |
| 1940 | 20 August | Trotsky assassinated in Mexico. |
| 1941 | 6 May | Stalin becomes Chairman of the Council of People's Commissars (Prime Minister) in place of Molotov. |

## The Soviet Union in the Great Fatherland War  German attack 22 June 1941 Page 47

| 1941 | 3 July | First public speech from Stalin after the German invasion. |
|------|--------|-----------------------------------------------------------|
|      | 7 August | Stalin names himself Commander-in-Chief. |
|      | 25 August | Siege of Leningrad begins. |
| 1942 | October — March | Battle of Moscow, won by Red Army. |
| 1943 | August — February | Battle of Stalingrad, won by Red Army. |
|      | 4-16 July | Battle of Kursk, won by Red Army. |
|      | 28 November — 1 December | Conference of Big Three at Tehran (Stalin, Roosevelt and Churchill). |
| 1944 | 27 January | Siege of Leningrad ends. |
|      | 22 June | Major offensive of Red Army in Byelorussia is very successful. |
|      | August | Red Army moves into Romania and Romania surrenders. Red Army also enters Bulgaria. |
|      | 19 September | Armistice signed with Finland (which had fought on the German side since June 1941). |
|      | Autumn | Red Army moves into Hungary, Yugoslavia and Poland. |
| 1945 | 4-11 February | Yalta Conference of the Big Three (Stalin, Roosevelt and Churchill). |
|      | 9 May | Victory in Europe Day. |
|      | 17-July-2 August | Potsdam Conference (Stalin, Truman, Churchill and Attlee). |
|      | 8 August | Soviet Union declares war on Japan. |
|      | 2 September | Japan surrenders. |

## After the War Pages 61-7

| 1946 | 9 February | Speech to election meeting in Moscow about the tasks ahead for the Soviet population. |
|------|-----------|---------------------------------------------------------------------------------------|
|      | 14 March | Reply to Churchill's comment about the "iron curtain" published in *Pravda*. |
| 1950 | 4 July | Views on *Marxism and Linguistics* published in *Pravda*. |
| 1951 | 2 September | Letter to Mao Tse-tung on anniversary of defeat of Japan |

|      |             | published in *Pravda*. |
|------|-------------|------------------------|
| 1952 | 1 February  | Completes last major work *Economic Problems of Socialism in the USSR* — not published in *Pravda* until 3 October 1952. |
|      | 14 October  | Last major public speech — at the 19th Congress of the Communist Party of the Soviet Union. |
|      | 21 December | Last interview appears in *Pravda* — an interview with James Reston of the *New York Times*. |
| 1953 | 5 March     | Dies. |

# Pseudonyms and Aliases of Joseph Vissarionovich Djugashvili (Stalin)

| Name | Nationality | Meaning | Used by |
|---|---|---|---|
| Soso | Georgian | Little Joseph | His mother |
| Soselo | Georgian | Dear little Joseph | His mother |
| Koba | Georgian | "the indomitable"; it is also the name of heroic outlaw in Georgian poem | Himself, as disguise from political police, 1902-13 |
| Ivanovich | Russian | — | Himself, as disguise from political police, December 1905 |
| Ko. | Georgian | short for Koba | Himself, as disguise from political police, 1906 |
| K. Kato | Georgian | — | Himself, as disguise from political police, 1907 |
| Gaioz Nizharadze | Georgian | — | Himself, as disguise, in Baku, 1907 |
| Chizhikov | Russian | — | Himself, as disguise in St Petersburg, 1911 |
| Vasilyev | Russian | — | Himself, as disguise, in St Petersburg, September 1912 |
| Zakhar Gregorian Melikyants | Armenian | — | Himself, as disguise, in Baku, 1909 |
| Stalin | Russian | Man of Steel | Himself, when signing an article in *Social Democrat*, a journal, in January 1913 |
| Vasily | Russian | — | Lenin, as code name for Stalin, February 1913 |
| K St. | Georgian-Russian | Koba Stalin | Himself, 1913 |
| J Besoshvili | Georgian | — | ) |
| David | Russian | — | ) all used as disguises to trick police |
| Ivanov | Russian | — | ) |
| Ryaboi | Russian | pock-marked | Police, as nickname |

# Biographical Notes on Stalin's Contemporaries

Page and picture references are given for mention of these people in the main text.

41 Bagramyan. An Armenian, he was a cavalry officer in the First World War, and had a good record in the Great Fatherland War as a field commander.

**Bagramyan**, Ivan Khristoforovich (1897-      ) was born in Kirovgrad. In 1920 he joined the Red Army and served in Transcaucasia until 1934. During the War he was Deputy Chief of Staff from 1941 to 1943, then Chief of Staff, South Western Front. He was Commander of the 11th Guards Army in 1943, Commander of the 1st Baltic Front in 1944 and Commander of the Baltic Military District 1945-54. (Page 55 and picture **41**)

**Beria**, Lavrenty Pavlovich (1899-1953) was born in Georgia. Having joined the Bolsheviks in 1917, he was important in the Communist Party of Georgia between 1931 and 1938. He became a member of the CC of the RCP(B) in 1934. He was head of the political police (**OGPU/NKVD**) 1938-53, and during the War was responsible for the police and for the production of ammunition. He joined the Politburo in 1946. He was arrested in June 1953 and executed in December 1953.

**Budyonny**, Semyon Mikhailovich (1883-1977) was born in Voronezh Province. He fought in the Russo-Japanese War (1904-5) and the First World War, then joined the Red Army and was Commander of the 1st Cavalry Army 1919-20. He was Inspector of the Red Army Cavalry 1924-37 and Commander of Moscow Military District 1937-39. He became a Marshal of the Soviet Union (the highest military rank) in 1935. He joined the Politburo in 1938. During the Great Fatherland War (1941-45) his record was surprisingly poor. (Page 53 and picture **32**)

**Bukharin,** Nikolai Ivanovich (1888-1938) was born in Moscow. He worked with Lenin from 1906 and became a member of the CC in 1917. He was Editor of the party newspaper *Pravda* 1918-28. He was a member of the Politburo 1919-29, and head of the Communist International (Comintern) 1926-29. His views were supported by Stalin in opposition to Trotsky, Kamenev and Zinoviev, but from 1928 Stalin attacked Bukharin. (See page 27.) In 1929 he was expelled from the Politburo and lost all his positions. He was executed on Stalin's orders. (Pages 16, 24, 26, 27-8, 41, 44, 45, 72, 73 and pictures 22, 51)

42   Dzerzhinsky, 1918. He was a strong supporter of Bukharin and the "Right", but died in July 1926, before the confrontation between Stalin and the "Right" opposition began.

43   Frunze reviews a parade of Red Army units, Ufa, 1919. He was one of the Red Army's military commanders during the Civil War.

**Dzerzhinsky,** Feliks Edmundovich (1877-1926) was born in Russian Poland. Having been active in social democratic politics, he became a member of the CC in August 1917. Lenin made him the first head of the political police (*Cheka*) in December 1917 and he remained in that post until his death. (Page 72 and picture **42**)

**Frunze,** Mikhail Vasilievich (1885-1925) was born in Pishpek, Turkestan. He joined the Bolsheviks in 1904 and was President of the Byelorussian Soviet in 1917. He played a leading role in the Civil War (1918-20) especially on the Urals and the Southern Fronts. He was Commander of the Red Army in the Ukraine in 1920 and became People's Commissar for War in January 1925. He died during a medical operation on 31 October 1925.

**Kamenev,** Lev Borisovich (1883-1936) was born in Moscow. A supporter of Lenin from 1903, he spent much time in exile in Siberia before 1917. He returned to Petrograd in April 1917 but was opposed to the October uprising. However, afterwards, he became Chairman of the Moscow Soviet 1918-22, and was a member of the Politburo from 1919 to 1925 and a candidate member January-October 1926. With Zinoviev and Stalin he opposed Trotsky as successor to Lenin in 1923, but after January 1925, when Stalin broke with the triumvirate, he sided with Trotsky. (See page 26.) He was expelled from the Politburo in October 1926 and expelled from the party in 1927. He was re-admitted to the party in 1928, expelled again in 1932, and executed on Stalin's orders. (Pages 9, 20, 24, 26, 27, 73, 74 and picture **44**)

**Khrushchev,** Nikita Sergeevich (1894-1970) was born in Kursk Province, the son of a coal miner. Having joined the Bolsheviks in 1918, he became a member of the CC in 1934, and

Secretary of the Moscow party organization 1935-38. Stalin gave him the job of carrying out the Great Purge (1936-38) in the Ukraine and because of his success made him a member of the Politburo in 1939. He was head of the party in the Ukraine until 1949 (except in 1947), and then became Secretary of the Moscow party organization again 1949-53. After Stalin's death he proved himself the most able politician, as head of the party (First Secretary) September 1953-October 1964, and also Prime Minister 1958-64. (Pages 45-6, 52, 53-5, 67 and picture **45**)

**Kirov**, Sergei Mironovich (1886-1934) was born in Vyatka Province, and was orphaned at the age of seven. Having joined the Bolsheviks in 1904, he helped to establish Soviet power in the Caucasus after 1917, and became a member of the CC in 1923. After Lenin's death, he supported Stalin, headed the important party organization in Leningrad, and joined the Politburo in 1930. His assassination on 1 December 1934 sparked off the Great Purge. Whether Stalin was responsible for his death is not certain. (Pages 41, 73, 74 and picture **46**)

**Lenin**, Vladimir Ilich (1870-1924), the founder of the Communist Party and the Soviet state, was born in Simbirsk (now Ulyanovsk), his real name being Vladimir Ilich Ulyanov. He was educated at the universities of Kazan and St Petersburg, where he

44  Kamenev. Always a moderate, he opposed
Trotsky, siding with Stalin, since the latter also
appeared a moderate. Once Trotsky had been defeated,
Stalin no longer needed Kamenev and Zinoviev, and
so he turned against them.

45  Khrushchev. A faithful ally of Stalin, especially ▷
in the Ukraine. He attacked Stalin only after the
latter was safely dead.

46  Kirov. The only real alternative to Stalin in 1934. His murder made Stalin politically safe.

obtained a first class degree in Law. The RSDLP was founded in 1898, and split in 1903, Lenin's followers becoming known as Bolsheviks, his opponents as Mensheviks. From 1906-14 he was mostly in Austria-Hungary and was in Switzerland during the First World War. He returned to Petrograd in April 1917 and immediately changed the policy of the Bolshevik party, urging the overthrow of the existing Provisional Government and a revolution. After the October uprising he became Chairman of People's Commissars (Prime Minister) as well as being the leading figure in the Communist Party. He was aware of the feud between Stalin and Trotsky, but did not live long enough to prevent one man destroying the other. Fanya Kaplan tried to assassinate Lenin on 30 August 1918, but none of the three bullets which entered his body killed him at the time. Kaplan's motives for trying to remove Lenin are unclear; she was executed immediately afterwards. One of the bullets lodged in Lenin's head and it was left there until the doctors decided to remove it on 23 April 1922. However, the operation caused Lenin to suffer a first stroke on 26 May 1922. He had a second stroke on 16 December 1922 and a third on 9 March 1923. (Pages 7, 9, 11, 12, 13, 14, 16, 17, 18, 19, 20, 21, 22, 23, 24, 67, 71, 72, 73 and pictures **1, 3, 4, 7, 9**)

**Litvinov**, Maksim Maksimovich (1876-1951) was born in Bialystok. Having joined the RSDLP in 1898, he became Lenin's secretary after his (Litvinov's) return to Russia in 1918. He was Deputy People's Commissar for Foreign Affairs 1918-29, People's Commissar for Foreign Affairs 1929-39 and Soviet Ambassador in Washington 1941-43. He was again Deputy People's Commissar for Foreign Affairs 1943-46, but lost favour with Stalin in 1946. (Page 74)

**Malenkov**, Georgy Maksimilianovich (1902- ) was born in Orenburg. Having joined the Communist Party in 1920, he worked in the CC and in the Moscow party organization 1925-39, and became a member of the CC in 1939. He played an important role in organizing war production 1941-45. In 1946 he became a full member of the Politburo, having been a candidate member since 1941, and was regarded as Stalin's successor. He was Prime Minister from March 1953 to February 1955, but lost his influence, due mainly to the superior political skill of Khrushchev. (Pages 52, 53, 55)

**Molotov**, Vyacheslav Mikhailovich (1890- ) was born in Vyatka Province. Having joined the Bolsheviks in 1906, he worked with Stalin on *Pravda* in 1912. He supported Stalin against Trotsky and joined the Politburo in 1926. From 1930-41 he was Chairman of the Council of People's Commissars (Prime Minister), and from 1939-49 and again from 1953-57 he was People's Commissar/Minister* for Foreign Affairs. He lost his influence when Khrushchev rose to political power. (Pages 73, 74 and picture **34**)

*People's Commissars were re-named Ministers in 1946.

Ordzhonikidze, Gregory Konstantinovich (1886-1937) was born in Georgia. Having joined the Bolsheviks in 1903, he became a member of the Petrograd Soviet in 1917. He was actively engaged in the Civil War (1918-20), then played an important part in establishing Soviet power in Armenia and Georgia in 1920 and 1921. He was acting on Stalin's behalf in the Georgian affair. (See page 18.) He became a member of the Politburo in 1930 and People's Commissar for Heavy Industry in 1932. He was on Stalin's side against Trotsky. (Page 18)

Timoshenko, Semyon Konstantinovich (1895-1977) Was born in the Ukraine. He fought in the First World War, then joined the Red

47  Timoshenko. His record was good as a field commander during the Great Fatherland War.

Army, and commanded forces in Byelorussia and the Ukraine 1933-40. He became a Marshal of the Soviet Union and People's Commissar for War in 1940. During the War he was responsible for the defence of the Ukraine. (Pages 48, 53 and picture 47)

Trotsky, Lev Davidovich (1879-1940) was born in the Ukraine, his real name being Lev Davidovich Bronstein. He was Chairman of the 1905 St Petersburg Soviet. Although he was critical of Lenin before 1917, he joined him after his return to Russia in 1917. As Chairman of the Military Revolutionary Committee of the Petrograd Soviet, he was the key figure in the October uprising. He organized the Red Army, and was the key military figure during the Civil War (1918-20). He joined the Politburo in 1919 and was expelled from it in 1926, as a result of the campaign against him which started with his writing of "Lessons of October" in 1924. (See page 24.) He was a brilliant speaker and writer, but a poor politician. He would have been Lenin's successor, had Stalin not taken action to prevent this. He was exiled to Soviet Central Asia in 1927 and was expelled from the Soviet Union, moving to Constantinople in 1929, then to Norway, and finally to Mexico City where he was assassinated, almost certainly, by one of Stalin's agents. (Pages 12, 14, 16, 17, 18, 19, 24, 26, 27, 71, 72, 73, 74 and picture 10)

Tukhachevsky, Mikhail Nikolaevich (1893-1937) was born in Smolensk Province. He fought as an officer in the First World War, then joined the Red Army. He was a brilliant commander during the Civil War (1918-20) but tasted defeat at Warsaw in 1920 during the Russo-Polish war (1918-21). With Trotsky he suppressed the Kronstadt revolt in March 1921 when sailors and workers at this naval base declared their opposition to the Communist Party. He was Chief of the Military Academy 1921-24, and Assistant Chief of Staff 1924-37. On 11 June 1937 he was

48 Tukhachevsky. One of the successes of the Civil War. Half French, his official contacts with the German Army (Reichswehr) before 1933 were used against him. Some of the material at his trial came from German counter-espionage.

cal police (Cheka). He became a member of the CC in 1921, and was People's Commissar for War 1925-34. He was on Stalin's side against Trotsky, and joined the Politburo 1926-52. From 1934-40 he was People's Commissar for War, and became a Marshal of the Soviet Union in 1935. From 1941-45 he was a member of the State Committee for Defence. (Page 53 and picture 49)

49 Voroshilov. Never popular with the professional soldiers, he was a political Marshal — Stalin's man among the military.

arrested and shot on Stalin's orders. In 1962 the state conceded that the charges against him had been false. (Page 74 and picture 48)

**Voroshilov,** Klementy Efrimovich (1881-1970) was born in the Ukraine. Having joined the Bolsheviks in 1903, he was a member of the Petrograd Soviet in 1917. He played an important part in the Civil War (1918-20). He helped Feliks Dzerzhinsky organize the politi-

**Zhukov,** Georgy Konstantinovich (1896-1977) was born in Kaluga Province. He joined the Communist Party in 1919. He fought in the Civil War (1918-20) and was in charge of Soviet defences in the Far East 1938-39. During the Great Fatherland War he was Chief of Staff of Soviet Forces, and organized the defences of Moscow in 1941 and of Stalingrad in 1942. He was the main driving force behind the Soviet advance to Berlin in early 1945. After the War he served in Germany but was then relegated to a minor post. It was said that Stalin was jealous of his popularity. After Stalin's death he served as Minister of Defence until 1957, when Khrushchev dismissed him. (Page 53 and picture **33**)

**Zinoviev,** Gregory Evseevich (1883-1936) was born in Elisavetgrad. He joined the Bolsheviks when the RSDLP was split in 1903 and returned with Lenin to Petrograd in Arpil 1917. Although he opposed the October uprising, he afterwards became Chairman of the Communist International (Comintern), and after Lenin's death was one of the triumvirate with Stalin and Kamenev who blocked Trotsky as successor to Lenin. After Stalin had broken with the triumvirate in January 1925, Zinoviev sided with Trotsky and was expelled from the Politburo, in July 1926. He was expelled from the party in 1927. He was arrested and shot on Stalin's orders. (Pages 9, 19-20, 23, 24, 26, 27, 72, 73, 74 and picture **8**)

# Glossary

AUCP(B) — All-Union Communist Party (Bolsheviks) (Page 73 )
The name of the Bolshevik Party from December 1925 to October 1952.

## Autonomous Republic
An area within a Soviet Republic where a nationality is concentrated which does not speak the language of the Soviet Republic (for example, Daghestan which is in the RSFSR and where the people are Daghestani and speak Daghestani as their first language). An Autonomous Republic has its own Soviet, its own government and its own constitution. In practice, this means very little, since the Autonomous Republic within the Soviet Republic is still firmly administered from the Republic's capital and that in turn is controlled by Moscow.

## Bolsheviks (Pages 7, 8, 9, 11, 12, 18, 21, 24, 70, 71)
The name (meaning those in the majority) of those members of the RSDLP who followed Lenin when he split the party in 1903. The Bolsheviks called their party successively the RSDLP (B), the All-Russian Communist Party (B), the All-Union Communist Party (Bolsheviks) and The Communist Party of the Soviet Union.

## CC — Central Committee (Pages 7, 12, 19, 24, 67, 71, 72, 73)
The Central Committee of the RSDLP. Such a body was first set up when the party was founded in 1898. A new Central Committee is elected at each congress, and that Central Committee then elects a Politburo.

## Central Control Commission
Set up in the communist party in 1920. Its task was to supervise the activities of the local control commissions. These local commissions had to examine complaints laid before them about "bureaucratic" behaviour of party workers, i.e. make sure that party officials behaved themselves and did not become little Tsars.

## Cheka (Page 78)
The political police. The name comes from the Russian initials for Extraordinary Commission. The full name of the organization was the Extraordinary Commission for the Struggle against Counterrevolution and Sabotage. The GPU (Main Political Administration) took over from the Cheka in February 1922, and the OGPU (Unified State Political Administration) took over from the GPU in 1923. In 1938 the GPU was merged with The People's Commissariat for Internal Affairs (NKVD). Now called the KGB.

## Collective see Kolkhoz

86

**Comintern** (Pages 23, 78, 85)
The Communist International, founded in 1919 and abolished in 1943. It consisted of all those communist and workers' parties which accepted the 21 conditions laid down (by Lenin) at the 2nd Comintern Congress in 1920.

**Commissar** (Pages 11, 12, 16, 24, 48, 53)
(i) a government minister, eg. Commissar of Foreign Affairs, or Minister of Foreign Affairs
(ii) top man at the local level; usually referred to as a government representative.
The term came to be used to mean a person holding considerable authority.

**Conference** (Pages 38, 71)
A meeting of party delegates from some parts of the country.

**Congress** (Pages 19, 22, 27, 45, 70, 71, 72, 73, 75 and picture 4)
A meeting of party delegates from all parts of the country. After 1917 there was usually a congress every year. The congress elects a new Central Committee and a new Politburo and decisions at the congress are binding on all members.

**Communist Party of the Soviet Union (CPSU)** (Pages 67, 75)
The name of the Bolshevik party since 1952.

**Duma** (Page 8)
Russian parliament between 1906 and 1917. The word comes from the Russian verb "to deliberate". Tsar Nicholas II issued the October Manifesto on 30 October (new style) 1905, providing for a Duma and political parties. A duma was based on restricted franchise and ran for five years. The first and second dumas had a much wider franchise than the third and fourth (1907-12 and 1912-1917). The fourth and last duma was dissolved on 27 February (old style) 1917. The Tsar feared it might usurp the power of his government.

**Emigré** (Pages 7, 29 and pictures **11** and **24**)
Person who is forced to live abroad because of his political views.

**Factionalism** (Pages 24, 41)
To the Bolshevik party this means opposing the party line. It is a term of abuse. If someone belonged to a group which was stated to oppose the party line (often this was untrue) he was accused of factionalism. Factionalism was formally banned at the 10th Party Congress in 1921. There could be no defence against a charge of factionalism, since it was the party which made the charge. Punishment can be expulsion from the party and possibly (especially in the · 1930s) death. Someone guilty of factionalism was called an "oppositionist".

**Five Year Plan** (Pages 27, 33, 41, 61, 62 and pictures **18** and **19**)
All economic activity is planned within a programme covering five years. The aims of the first Five Year Plan were achieved in four years and three months, October 1928-32. The second FYP ran from 1933-37, the third from 1938-41. The USSR is now (1979) in its tenth FYP.

**Great Fatherland War (1941-45)** (Chapter 4)
The Second World War began on 1 September 1939, when Germany attacked Poland. The Soviet Union also attacked Poland, on 17 September 1939. Germany and the Soviet Union had concluded a non-aggression pact on 23 August 1939 (an agreement not to attack each other) and they were therefore not in danger of fighting over Poland. However, on 22 June 1941 Germany did attack the Soviet Union, and this began the Great Fatherland War. It lasted until 9 May 1945. (When Germany surrendered on 8 May 1945, late in the evening, it was already 9 May 1945 in Moscow, since Moscow is to the east of Berlin.) After the German attack on the Soviet Union, Great Britain and the Soviet Union became allies against Germany, and they were joined

by the USA in 1941, after the Japanese attack on Pearl Harbour and the German declaration of war against the USA. Since they defeated Germany, Great Britain, the USA and the USSR are referred to as the Great Powers. France, who joined the war in 1944, also played a part in defeating Germany. She is also referred to as a Great Power.

## Illegal political activities (under the Tsar) (Page 7)

When a person was tried for illegal political activity and the judge considered that criminal activity had been proved, the accused was sent to prison. If the only evidence of political activity was that of the Tsarist political or secret police, and illegal political activity could not be proved to the judge's satisfaction, then the accused was "exiled" (sent a long way away). This was called "administrative exile". Under a Tsarist law, "dangerous people" were "administratively exiled" when it was thought that they *might* cause trouble for the authorities if they continued to live where they were.

## Izvestiya

The Government newspaper. It started off as the *Izvestiya* of the Petrograd Soviet, was then the *Izvestiya* of the Central Executive Committee of the Soviets, then the *Izvestiya* of the government. The word "izvestiya" means news.

## KGB (Page 45)

The Committee of State Security. The present-day name of the political police. (*See* Cheka, NKVD, OGPU).

## Kolkhoz (Pages 27, 31, 34, 36, 37, 38, 51, 61 and picture 14)

A collective farm where all the land is worked by all the peasants in common. Until 1966 the collective farm peasants were paid only after the harvest. If the harvest was good they did well. If the harvest was poor they got little. Hence no one could be sure that he would receive much money in the autumn. In 1966 a minimum monthly wage was introduced but the majority of a kolkhoznik's income still depends on the size of the harvest.

## Kulak (Pages 26, 27, 34, 36)

The word "kulak" means fist, and was used as an uncomplimentary word for money-lenders. Rich peasants who exploited others were called kulaks. In his *Development of Capitalism in Russia* of 1898 Lenin popularized the idea that the peasantry was divided into three groups: the well-off, the middle and the poor. The term he used for well-off peasant was not an abusive one and meant simply one who had plenty to live on. After 1917 the abusive word "kulak" was attached to the richer peasants, and then came to be used for anyone who opposed collectivization.

The word "kulak" has now entered the English language and it has been used in Tanzania to describe (with an abusive connotation, of course) those peasants who did not favour collectives.

## Marxism (Pages 7, 23, 24, 65, 70)

The teachings of Karl Marx. They fall under the headings of Philosophy, Economics, Politics and Sociology.

On politics, he wrote that the state and the capitalist system were exploitative. Labour (work done) was the true source of value. Revolution was necessary to remove those who owned the factories and other property and to place the ownership of the means of production (factories, etc) in the hands of the workers. The revolution which would abolish capitalism would be socialist, and it was inevitable. After the socialist revolution there would be a short phase called the dictatorship of the proletariat, during which the working class would defeat the attempts of the capitalists to recapture power. After this violent period peace would reign and the true potential of each person would be realized. Marx believed that under socialism there would be a very high standard of living. Eventually money would disappear and a paradise on earth would prevail. Marx rejected all forms of religion and did not accept the existence of supernatural powers. To him, a socialist was also an atheist.

## Mensheviks (Pages 8, 27)
The name (meaning those in the minority) of those members of the RSDLP who opposed Lenin when he split the party in 1903.

## NEP — New Economic Policy (Pages 26, 41)
This was inaugurated at the 10th Party Congress in March 1921 and ran until the beginning of the first Five Year Plan. Under NEP the commanding heights of the economy (heavy industry, key defence industries) stayed in the state sector, while light industry reverted to the market economy and private ownership. Foreigners could take out concessions and take over a factory from the government. For example, one American took over a factory in Moscow and produced top hats for the world market.

Agriculture, under NEP, almost totally reverted to the pre-June 1918 era. The peasants were allowed to market their grain again and the market for food was legal once more.

Traders who took advantage of the times were known as Nepmen (page 26).

## NKVD (Page 77)
The People's Commissariat of Internal Affairs. Sometimes the Cheka functions were carried out by the NKVD. Hence the NKVD was at certain times the internal police force and the political police force. At present, the MVD (Ministry of Internal Affairs) is responsible for the civilian police only and the KGB (Committee for State Security) for the political police.

## OGPU (Page 77)
The Unified State Political Administration (political police), set up in 1923. (See Cheka).

## Oppositionist (Pages 24, 27, 41)
Someone accused by the Bolshevik party (sometimes quite unfairly) of opposing the existing party line. (See factionalism.) The greatest blow to any top communist (someone who had devoted his whole life to the party and its success) was to be called an oppositionist. Such was the emotional and psychological shock of being called an anti-party man that many (including Bukharin) broke down and wept and pleaded for forgiveness.

## Order of the Red Banner (Page 16 and picture 50)
A military decoration for those persons who have displayed outstanding courage and bravery in battle. It was created by the Sovnarkom on 16 December 1918 and is still awarded today. The decoration is a round badge with a banner and flag, and the inscription "Workers of the World Unite" on the bottom. This same slogan appears at the top left-hand corner of Pravda. Today the badge is worn attached to a red and white cloth pennant.

50 The Order of the Red Banner worn by Pyotr Katsereyev, from Rostov-on-Don, for efficient work as a navigator at sea.

**Orgburo** (Page 12)
The Organizational Bureau of the Central Committee of the Communist Party, formed in March 1919 and abolished in October 1952. It was originally a sub-committee of the Central Committee but quickly usurped some of the powers of the CC. It worked closely with the Politburo, and these two institutions gradually took the key party decisions.

**Petrograd Soviet of Workers' and Soldiers' Deputies** (Pages 7, 9)
The full name of the Petrograd Soviet (or council) gives the impression that only soldiers and workers were allowed to elect and be elected to it. This is not true, however. Lawyers and other professional people were also elected to the Petrograd Soviet set up in March 1917, and it represented almost everyone in Petrograd. The ordinary person turned to the Soviet when he had a problem and this is why the Petrograd Soviet is referred to as a "government". As well as the city-wide Petrograd Soviet, each borough of Petrograd had its own Soviet.

The 1917 Petrograd Soviet was not the first to have existed in Petrograd; there had been one during the 1905 revolution.

**Politburo** (Pages 12, 18, 19, 27, 72, 73)
The Political Bureau — the supreme body of the Communist Party, founded at the 8th Congress of the RCP(B) in March 1919. It is

51 Bukharin and Maria Ulyanova, Lenin's sister, working on *Pravda*, 1924.

elected anew at each Congress by the newly elected Central Committee. Today the Politburo contains all the key figures in party and government life in the Soviet Union.

## Pravda (Pages 7, 22, 23, 29, 64-5, 66, 67, 71, 72, 74, 75 and picture 51)

The newspaper of the Russian Communist Party. It first appeared as a legal paper on 5 May (new style) 1912. It is the organ of the Central Committee of the party. The word "Pravda" means truth.

Between 1912-14 *Pravda* was printed in 40,000-60,000 copies daily. Of the 645 issues between 1912-14, 190 were confiscated by the Tsarist police. However, the paper appeared under other names, eg. *Workers' Pravda*, *Northern Pravda*, *Labour Pravda*, etc. The paper was closed down by the Imperial Government on 8 July 1914.

The next issue appeared on 18 March 1917, and in the summer of that year 90,000 copies were produced daily. On 18 July 1917 the printing presses were smashed, but the paper appeared under other names, eg. *Worker and Soldier*. *Pravda* appeared again under its own name on 9 November 1917.

In 1975 10.6 million copies of *Pravda* were sold daily, the largest sale of any newspaper in the USSR.

One of *Pravda*'s most famous editors was Nikolai Bukharin during the 1920s.

## Provisional Government (Pages 7, 8, 9)

When the Duma was dissolved in March 1917, some of its members formed a Provisional or Temporary Government. This was the official government as opposed to the unofficial Petrograd Soviet. It was called Provisional since it was a caretaker government only for the time until the Constituent Assembly (parliament) was elected. The Provisional Government changed four times between March and November 1917. The Prime Minister in the first two PGs was Prince G.E. Lvov, who did not belong to any political party. The Prime Minister in the last two PGs

was Alexander Kerensky, a Socialist Revolutionary. There were only ten ministers in the first PG, but seventeen in the last.

## Purge (Pages 19, 41, 51)

Usually purges (getting rid of undesirable members) were carried out in the party. Two methods were used. It might be ordered that all members re-register; and then membership would be refused to those people not wanted. Or the unwanted members would be simply expelled from the party. During the 1930s there were purges in every sector of Soviet life (eg. in the Government, the Party, the Army, etc.)

## RCP(B) — All-Russian Communist Party (Bolsheviks) (Pages 12, 18, 19, 21, 23, 27 and picture 4)

The name of the Bolshevik party between March 1918 and December 1925, when it was renamed the All-Union Communist Party (Bolsheviks).

## Red Army (Pages 12, 13, 14, 16, 17, 31, 37, 48, 50, 51, 52, 53, 55, 56, 58, 59, 61, 67 and pictures 30, 43 and 52)

The full name of the army was the Workers' and Peasants' Red Army. Red (the colour of blood) is the symbol of the Bolshevik party and of socialist parties in Europe before. The army was set up in early 1918. It was renamed the Soviet Army during the Great Fatherland War.

## Republic (Pages 11, 18, 22, 29, and picture 39)

A state where the top person is a civilian, and not a king or queen. Russia became a republic under the Provisional Government (i.e. the monarchy had disappeared before the October Revolution). To start with, Soviet Russia was the (one) Soviet Republic. Then came the Ukrainian Soviet Republic, then the Byelorussian Soviet Republic, then the Transcauscasian Soviet Republic. Today there are 15 republics which together form the Soviet Union.

**RSDLP — The Russian Social Democratic Labour Party** (Pages 7, 8)
Founded in 1898. Based its strength on the industrial workers. The party was split by Lenin in 1903, those members following him taking the name of Bolsheviks, and his opponents within the party taking the name of Mensheviks. Until 1918 when the Bolsheviks changed their name to Russian Communist Party (Bolsheviks), the RSDLP included both Bolsheviks and Mensheviks.

**RSDLP(B) — The Russian Social Democratic Labour Party (Bolsheviks)**
At the 7th Conference of the RSDLP in May 1917 the Bolshevik section of the party added the word "Bolsheviks" in brackets to the party name, to distinguish themselves from the rest of the party.

52  An unusual picture of the Red Army. In a campaign to combat malaria, every Red Army soldier was made to drink quinine. To sweeten the bitter ceremony, a military orchestra plays to the soldiers.

**RSFSR — Russian Soviet Federated (or Federative) Socialist Republic** (Page 18)
Formed on 10 July 1918 and referred to as "a republic of Soviets of Workers', Soldiers' and Peasants' Deputies". Also referred to as Soviet Russia.

**Rubles**
Unit of Russian (pre-1917) and Soviet currency. In 1917 there were 10 rubles to a pound (£).

**Secretariat**
Body responsible for all the administrative work of the Central Committee and the

Politburo of the Communist Party. The Secretariat is elected by the Central Committee.

## Secretary General (Pages 12, 19, 20, 73)

Head of the Secretariat. During Lenin's lifetime the job was not regarded as the most important in the party. After Lenin's death, Stalin made it the leading post in the party. After Stalin's death, the top party official became known as the First Secretary. The present head of the party, Leonid Ilich Brezhnev, has reverted to the former title, Secretary General.

## Soviet (Pages 7, 22, 23, 53, 56, 79)

Russian word for council. The word is used in this way in the text. But "Soviet" also describes the country: for example, Soviet government, the Soviet Union, a Soviet citizen.

## Sovnarkom (Pages 9, 11, 71)

Short for Sovet Narodnikh Kommissarov — the Soviet or Council of People's Commissars. It was the name adopted by the first Bolshevik government in 1918. They wanted a new name for the government, which sounded different, so that the average person would be convinced that something had changed. Trotsky coined the name "Sovnarkom", and Lenin liked it, so the name was adopted.

## SRP — The Socialist Revolutionary Party (Page 8)

The main agrarian party which wanted peasants to have land without paying rent. Members were called SRs — Socialist Revolutionaries.

## State Planning Commission (Page 41)

The organization which draws up the Five Year Plans, annual plans, etc. It was, and still is, responsible for the entire economic activity of the Soviet Union.

## Supreme Soviet (Pages 28, 67 and picture 11)

The Supreme Soviet, according to the 1977 Constitution, is the "highest organ of state power in the USSR". It was established in 1936 as a result of the Constitution of 1936. It is bicameral (has two houses) and the houses are co-equal. The houses are the Soviet of the Union and the Soviet of Nationalities. The former is elected on the basis of population, the latter on a territorial basis by nationality unit (32 deputies from a Union republic, 11 from an Autonomous Republic, etc.).

## USSR — Union of Soviet Socialist Republics (Pages 18, 67)

Came into being on 31 January 1924, and consisted then of four states: RSFSR, Ukraine, Byelorussia and Transcaucasia). It expanded in 1925 to include the Turkmen and Uzbek Autonomous Republics, which had been elevated to full Union status within the USSR. The Tadzhik Autonomous Republic followed suit in 1929. Meanwhile, the Transcaucasian Soviet Federated Republic (to give Transcaucasia its full name) was divided into the republics of Azerbaidzhan, Armenia and Georgia. Hence, by 1929 the USSR consisted of nine republics.

## White Army (Pages 12, 16)

The Army which opposed the Reds in the Civil War. The Bolsheviks called the Whites "White Guardists", a term of abuse. The term has nothing to do with Byelorussia, which means "White Russia".

The Whites were the main military opponents of the Reds, but there were also the Greens or anarchists. Their leader was Nestor Makhno, who survived the Civil War and died in Paris in 1936. The Greens (the colour of grass) were so called because they wanted the peasants to be left in peace and to set up self-governing communities — unmolested by governments of all hues.

# Some Suggestions for Further Reading

| | | |
|---|---|---|
| Brian Catchpole | *A Map History of Russia* | Heinemann |
| B.W. Caws and R.F. Watts | *The Earthquake Hour: A Scrapbook of the Second World War* | Blackie |
| David Childs | *Marx and the Marxists* | Ernest Benn |
| M. Gibson | *Russia under Stalin* | Wayland |
| Hayes & Gregory | *Joseph Stalin* | Wayland |
| Robert Hoare | *World War One* | Macdonald |
| Robert Hoare | *World War Two* | Macdonald |
| L.F. Hobley | *The Second World War* | Blackie |
| N.C. Jackson | *Russia in the Twentieth Century* | Wheaton |
| John Kennett | *The Growth of Modern Russia* | Blackie |
| E. Koutaissoff | *Soviet Union* | Ernest Benn |
| Peter Lane | *The USSR in the Twentieth Century* | Batsford |
| Sally Pickering | *20th-Century Russia* | Oxford |
| J.D. Reid | *A Visual History of Russia* | Evans |
| R.B. Rose | *The Russian Revolution* | Frederick Warne |
| F.W. Stacey | *Stalin and the Making of Modern Russia* | Edward Arnold |
| R.J. Unstead | *Incredible Century* | Macdonald |
| R.J. Unstead | *The Twenties* | Macdonald |
| R.J. Unstead | *The Thirties* | Macdonald |
| Stephen White | *The USSR: Portrait of a Superpower* | Blackie |

# Visual Aids

*The End of Tsarism, 1857-1917*
(Ref. L 743) Distributed by the Slide Centre, for Longman

*The General Line*
112-minute silent Russian film of 1929 — a study of the conflict between old and new styles of farming, and the policy of New Soviet Society with its co-operative farming and mechanized techniques. (From British Film Institute)

*Georgi Zhukov, Marshal of the Soviet Union*
50-foot colour film. Includes Zhukov's clashes with Stalin (BBC)

*Land of the Soviets*
60-minute silent film about British Communist Party Delegation visiting Russia, 1935 (includes shots of Stalin, Voroshilov, Kalinin, Molotov and Kaganovich) (Stanley Forman)

*Leningrad*
35mm filmstrip on Leningrad past and present (Gateway Educational Media Ref FGGP/47)

*Leningrad*
Silent loop film on Leningrad past and present (Gateway Educational Media Ref GGP/757)

*Moscow*
35mm filmstrip on modern Moscow (Gateway Educational Media, Ref. FGGP/46)

*Moscow*
Silent loop film of Moscow past and present (Gateway Educational Media Ref. GGP/756)

*Moscow to Peking*
Sound film showing a train journey across Asia, showing Moscow, Ural Mountains, Siberia, new industrial towns, Lake Baikal, then on through Mongolia and China (Gateway Educational Media Ref 206)

*The Revolution Will Not Now Take Place*
50-foot black and white film about impact of Communist ideas in Europe from the Bolshevik Revolution to the present day (BBC)

*Russia — An Introduction*
Sound film about history from Peter the Great to October Revolution, showing people in everyday situations (Gateway Educational Media Ref 196)

*Russia — Background to History I and II*
Silent loop films, I about pre-revolutionary conditions, II post-revolution, including shots of Stalin (Gateway Educational Media Refs HGP/759 and HGP/760)

*Russia — Background to History I and II*
35 mm filmstrips, I of scenes providing back-

ground to famous events in Russian history, and II providing background to the lives of the Russian people of the past (Gateway Educational Media, Refs FHGP/49 and FHGP/50)

*Soviet Russia 1918-1964*
Ref L2031 Distributed by the Slide Centre for Longman

*The Superpowers*
Unit 2 of "History 1917-1971", 20-foot black and white film for 14-16-year-olds. "The Superpowers" consists of 6: Lenin's Revolution; 7: Stalin's Revolution; 8: Khrushchev and the Thaw; 9: America gets involved; 10: The Cold War (BBC)

*World Leaders: Stalin: Man of Steel*
60-minute colour sound film (For sale from Seabourne Enterprises Ltd. For hire from Film Forum (dbw) Ltd)

*World War I: Eastern Fronts*
12 slides, scenes of some of the Eastern Fronts — Balkans/Russia — landing at Salonika/Gallipoli/Palestine (Slide Centre Ltd Ref S671)

*World War I: Commanders of the Fighting Forces*
12 slides of French, Russian and Italian commanders (The Slide Centre Ltd Ref S859)

*World War II: Commanders of the Fighting Forces*
12 slides of the Russian Commanders (The Slide Centre Ltd Ref S955)

## Index

The Index for this book is incorporated into the *Biographical Notes on Stalin's Contemporaries* (page 77) and the *Glossary* (page 86). Both these sections are arranged alphabetically.

To look up a particular person, go to the *Biographical Notes* (page 77) and you will find details about that person, plus a list of pages on which he is also mentioned.

To look up a subject, such as Bolsheviks, Five Year Plan or Red Army, go to the *Glossary* (page 86) and you will find details about that subject and a list of pages on which it is also mentioned.